GREATEST SPORTS MOMENTS

LAKE PLACID
MIRACLE
WHEN U.S. HOCKEY
STUNNED THE WORLD

BY BLAKE HOENA
ILLUSTRATED BY EDUARDO GARCIA AND RED WOLF STUDIO

CONSULTANT:
BRUCE BERGLUND
PROFESSOR OF HISTORY, CALVIN COLLEGE
GRAND RAPIDS, MICHIGAN

CAPSTONE PRESS
a capstone imprint

Graphic Library is published by Capstone Press,
1710 Roe Crest Drive, North Mankato, Minnesota 56003
www.mycapstone.com

Library of Congress Cataloging-in-Publication data
Names: Hoena, B. A., author. | Garcia, Eduardo, 1970 August 31- illustrator.
Title: Lake Placid miracle : when U. S. hockey stunned the world / by Blake Hoena ; illustrated by Eduardo Garcia.
   Other titles: 1980 US hockey team. | 1980 United States hockey team.
Description: North Mankato, Minnesota : Graphic Library, an imprint of Capstone Press, [2018] |
   Series: Graphic Library. Greatest Sports Moments | Includes index. | Audience: Ages: 8–14.
Identifiers: LCCN 2018001971 (print) | LCCN 2018007830 (ebook) | ISBN 9781543528756 (eBook PDF) |
   ISBN 9781543528671 (hardcover) | ISBN 9781543528718 (paperback)
Subjects: LCSH: Hockey—United States—History—20th century—Juvenile literature. | Olympic Winter Games
   (13th : 1980 : Lake Placid, N.Y.)—Juvenile literature. | Hockey teams—United States—Juvenile literature.
Classification: LCC GV848.4.U6 (ebook) | LCC GV848.4.U6 H87 2018 (print) | DDC 796.98—dc23
LC record available at https://lccn.loc.gov/2018001971

Summary: Tells the story of the Miracle on Ice game between the U.S. and U.S.S.R. men's Olympic hockey teams at the 1980 Olympic Games at Lake Placid, New York.

EDITOR
Aaron J. Sautter

ART DIRECTOR
Nathan Gassman

DESIGNER
Ted Williams

MEDIA RESEARCHER
Eric Gohl

PRODUCTION SPECIALIST
Laura Manthe

Direct quotations appear in **bold italicized text** on the following pages:

Page 4 (panel 4): from "July 20, 1969: One Giant Leap For Mankind," by NASA, July 20, 2017 (https://www.nasa.gov/mission_pages/apollo/apollo11.html).
Page 6 (panel 2), page 14 (panel 1): from "Spongecoach's Best Herb Brooks Quotes: 29 Inspiring Herb Brooks Quotes to Motivate You," by Spongecoach, September 13, 2017 (http://www.spongecoach.com/inspiring-herb-brooks-quotes/).
Page 25: from "'Do You Believe in Miracles? YES!' ... We Did During USA Hockey Team's Run to Gold Medal" by Steven Marcus, Newsday, February 22, 2015 (https://www.newsday.com/sports/hockey/do-you-believe-in-miracles-yes-we-did-during-usa-hockey-team-s-run-to-gold-medal-1.9963102).
Page 26 (panel 2): from Herb Brooks: Gold Medal Game (http://herbbrooks1980.weebly.com/gold-medal-game.html).

Printed and bound in the United States of America.
PA017

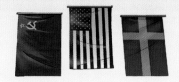

TABLE OF CONTENTS

THE COLD WAR

After World War II (1939–1945) the United States and the Soviet Union were at odds with one another.

Each super power believed its form of government was best and tried to influence other countries around the world. Their long conflict became known as the Cold War (1947–1991).

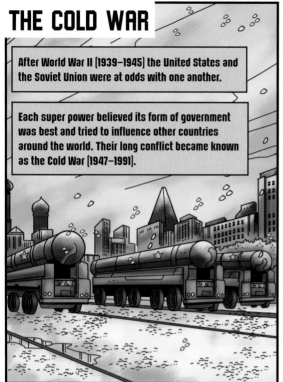

After the first nuclear bombs were developed in the 1940s, the two powers entered an arms race. Each country sought to have the most powerful nuclear weapons.

After launching spacecraft in the 1950s, the two countries entered the space race. On April 12, 1961, the Soviet Union launched the *Vostok I* spacecraft. Yuri Gagarin became the first person to enter space and orbit the Earth.

We wish you a good flight, Yuri.

On July 16, 1969, the United States launched a *Saturn V* rocket with three astronauts onboard, Michael Collins, Buzz Aldrin, and Neil Armstrong. On July 21, Neil Armstrong became the first person to ever walk on the Moon.

That's one small step for a man, one giant leap for mankind.

Tensions between the two countries were even felt on the Olympic hockey rink.

The Soviets have beaten the U.S. team to win the 1956 Olympic gold medal.

The 1960 U.S. Hockey team has just won the gold!

During the 1960s and 1970s the Soviet team completely dominated the Olympic competition.

1964, Innsbruck, Austria

1968, Grenoble, France

1972, Sapporo, Japan

1976, Innsbruck, Austria

The Soviets have won gold in four straight Olympics. I don't know if anyone will ever stop this team.

But in 1980, a tough coach and a group of scrappy young players were about to shock the world . . .

5

BUILDING A TEAM

Olympic Hockey Tryouts, Bloomington, Minnesota, 1979.

They couldn't have picked a better coach, Herb. After winning three NCAA National Championships, now you finally get your chance to win Olympic gold.

I can't believe they cut you from the U.S. team back in 1960.

Yeah, Coach Riley had to make some tough decisions to build the team back then. We'll have to do the same thing with these college kids.

Herb Brooks and his assistant coach, Craig Patrick, selected players they felt fit with their strategy.

I'm not looking for the best players. I'm looking for the right ones. I want guys who can play smart. We need to focus on teamwork, passing, and conditioning. It's the only way we'll compete against the European teams and the Soviets.

I've coached Buzz Schneider before. I know what he can bring to our team.

Mark Johnson is fast, and one of Wisconsin's top scorers.

Jim Craig has the fire to win. He's been an amazing goalie at Boston University.

Once Brooks had chosen his team, he put them to work . . . and he worked them hard.

Come on! Pick it up! To compete with the best in the world, you need to skate like the best in the world!

Brooks pushed his players to play the type of hockey he felt would win games.

Come on! Pass it! Pass it! Heroics don't win games . . . teamwork does!

Leading up to the Olympics, the U.S. team played in 61 exhibition games, finishing with a record of 42–16–3. These games helped Brooks' team sharpen their skills to compete against the world's toughest competition.

7

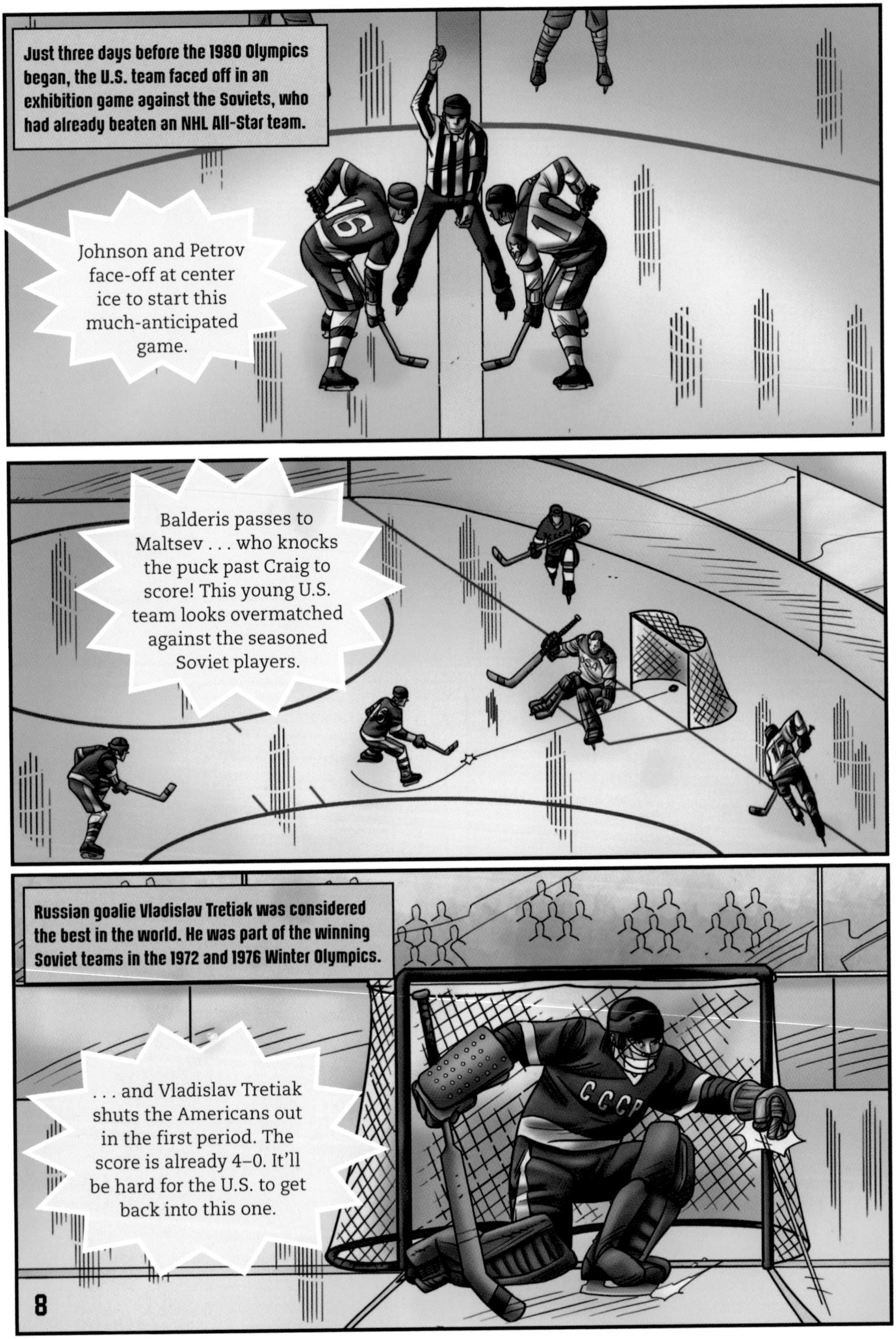
Just three days before the 1980 Olympics began, the U.S. team faced off in an exhibition game against the Soviets, who had already beaten an NHL All-Star team.
Johnson and Petrov face-off at center ice to start this much-anticipated game.
Balderis passes to Maltsev . . . who knocks the puck past Craig to score! This young U.S. team looks overmatched against the seasoned Soviet players.
Russian goalie Vladislav Tretiak was considered the best in the world. He was part of the winning Soviet teams in the 1972 and 1976 Winter Olympics.
. . . and Vladislav Tretiak shuts the Americans out in the first period. The score is already 4–0. It'll be hard for the U.S. to get back into this one.
CCCP

The United States scored a goal in the second period, but the game didn't get much better for them.

Vladimir Krutov scores his third goal for the hat trick, extending the Soviets' lead!

The Soviets embarrassed the U.S. team 10–3. Although the Soviet players were officially considered amateurs, they were as good as any pro team. They had sharpened their skills in a world-class league and played at a high level of competition.

	1	2	3	
USA	0	1	2	03
USSR	4	2	4	10

GETTING TO THE FINALS

The 1980 Olympic hockey tournament began with group play. Teams played against each team in their division.

Blue Division		Red Division
• Czechoslovakia		• Canada
• Norway		• Finland
• Romania		• Japan
• Sweden		• Netherlands
• West Germany		• Poland
• United States		• Soviet Union

We have to play Sweden first. And then Czechoslovakia. Both are serious medal contenders.

We have a tough draw, but I believe we can finish in the top two in our division. That'll get us to the medal round.

February 12, 1980. U.S.A. vs. Sweden.

. . . Berglund has the puck and passes to Molin . . .

. . . Molin gives it to Andersson, who takes a shot and scores! Team Sweden gets on the board first.

In the third period, Sweden had taken a 2–1 lead. With less then a minute left in the game, Brooks made a desperate move.

What's this? Brooks has pulled Craig from the goal, giving team USA six skaters on the ice. Schneider fights for the puck near the boards . . .

. . . the pass is to Baker, who takes a shot at the goal . . .

Wow! Baker ties up the game with just 27 seconds to go!

An early loss could have dashed the U.S. team's chances of reaching the medal round. But the 2–2 tie with Sweden kept their hopes alive.

Baker's key goal against Sweden put a spark into the U.S. team. In the next game the team beat Czechoslovakia, which had been favored to win the silver medal.

The team went on to win its next three games in group play.

SCORE
USA 7 TCH 3

SCORE
USA 5 NOR 1

SCORE
USA 7 ROU 3

SCORE
USA 4 FRG 2

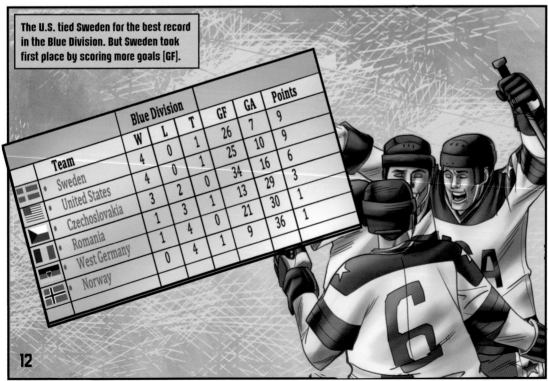

The U.S. tied Sweden for the best record in the Blue Division. But Sweden took first place by scoring more goals (GF).

Team	Blue Division			GF	GA	Points
	W	L	T			
Sweden	4	0	1	26	7	9
United States	4	0	1	25	10	9
Czechoslovakia	3	2	0	34	16	6
Romania	1	3	1	13	29	3
West Germany	1	4	0	21	30	1
Norway	0	4	1	9	36	1

Meanwhile, the Soviet team dominated in the Red Division. The Soviets started by demolishing Japan 16–0. Their impressive wins didn't stop there.

SCORE
URS 17 | NED 4

SCORE
URS 8 | POL 1

SCORE
URS 4 | FIN 2

SCORE
URS 6 | CAN 4

The Soviets went undefeated in the Red Division. Finland tied Canada's record. But Finland had defeated Canada in head-to-head competition to take second place.

The medal round was set. Sweden, the United States, the Soviet Union, and Finland would battle for Olympic gold.

Team	Red Division			GF	GA	Points
	W	L	T			
Soviet Union	5	0	0	51	11	10
Finland	3	2	0	26	18	6
Canada	3	2	0	28	12	6
Poland	2	3	0	15	23	4
Netherlands	1	3	1	16	43	3
Japan	0	4	1	7	36	1

THE MIRACLE

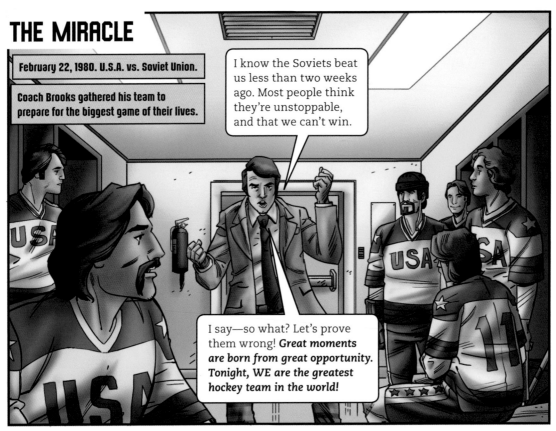

February 22, 1980. U.S.A. vs. Soviet Union.

Coach Brooks gathered his team to prepare for the biggest game of their lives.

I know the Soviets beat us less than two weeks ago. Most people think they're unstoppable, and that we can't win.

I say—so what? Let's prove them wrong! *Great moments are born from great opportunity. Tonight, WE are the greatest hockey team in the world!*

U-S-A! U-S-A! U-S-A!

The stands here at the Olympic Arena are packed tonight. Thousands of hockey fans are here to see the upstart U.S. team take on the undefeated Soviets.

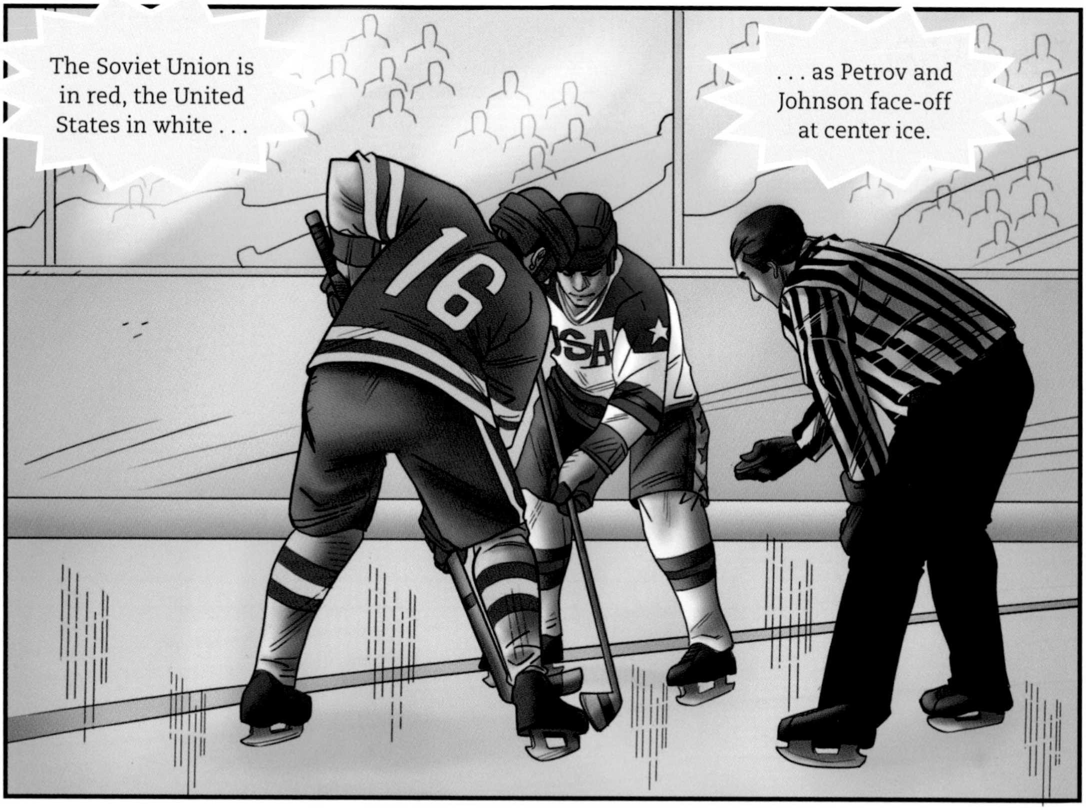
The Soviet Union is in red, the United States in white . . .
. . . as Petrov and Johnson face-off at center ice.

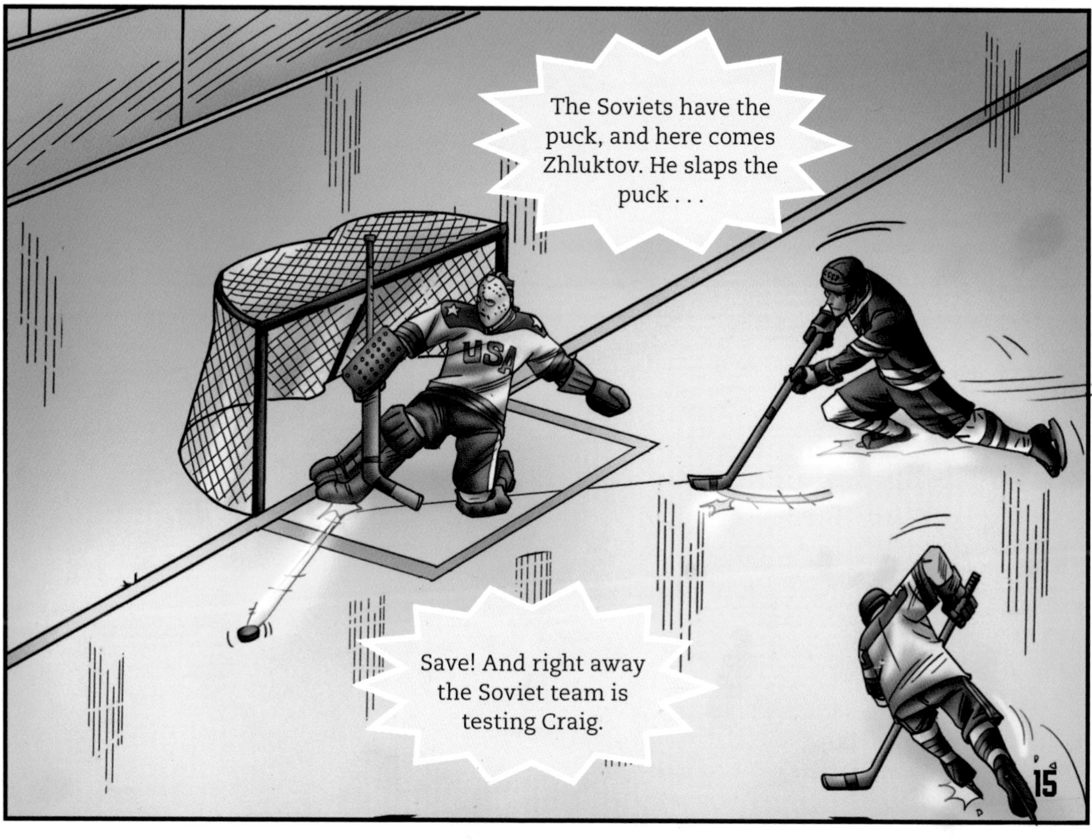
The Soviets have the puck, and here comes Zhluktov. He slaps the puck . . .
Save! And right away the Soviet team is testing Craig.

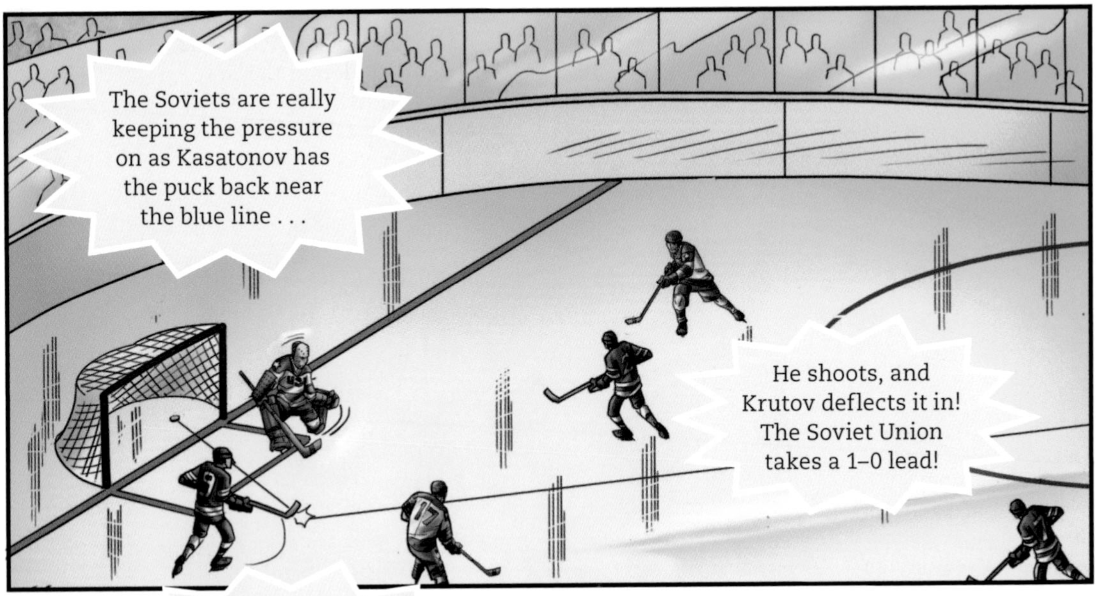
The Soviets are really keeping the pressure on as Kasatonov has the puck back near the blue line . . .
He shoots, and Krutov deflects it in! The Soviet Union takes a 1–0 lead!

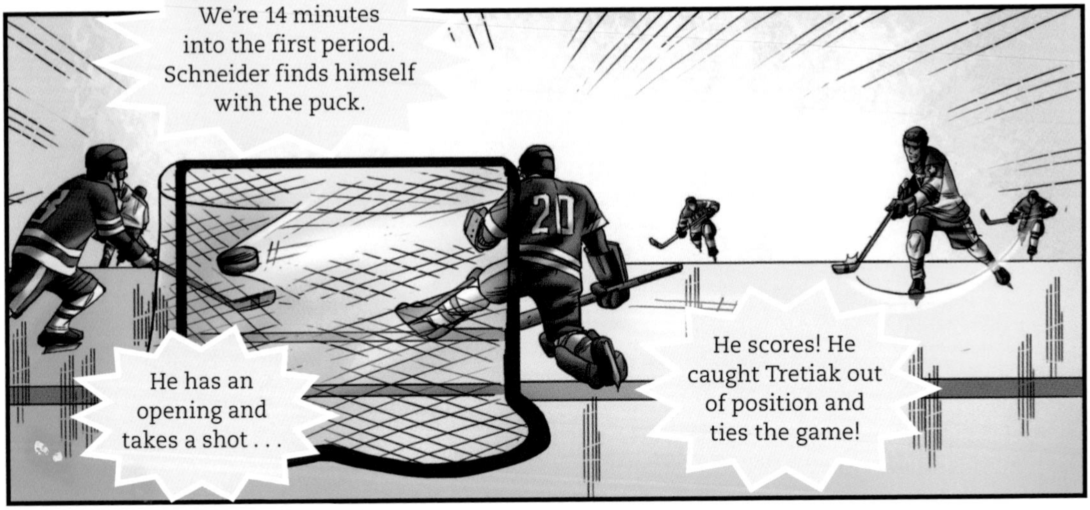
We're 14 minutes into the first period. Schneider finds himself with the puck.
He has an opening and takes a shot . . .
He scores! He caught Tretiak out of position and ties the game!

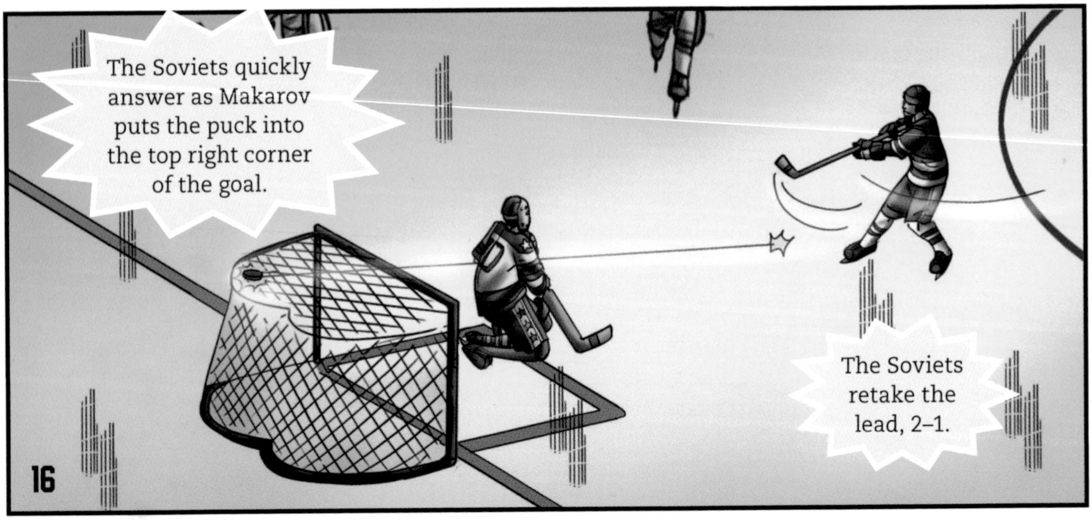
The Soviets quickly answer as Makarov puts the puck into the top right corner of the goal.
The Soviets retake the lead, 2–1.

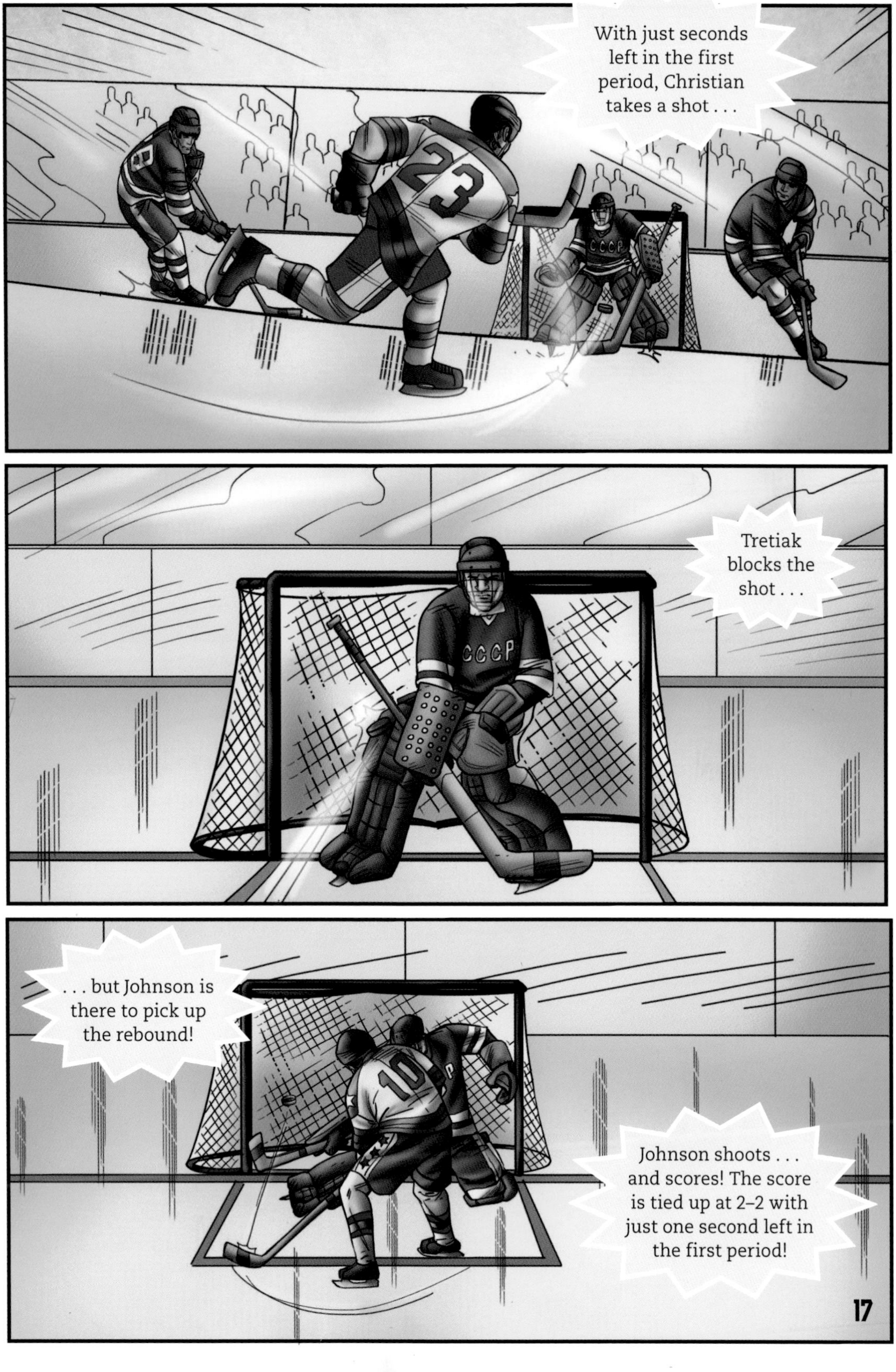
With just seconds left in the first period, Christian takes a shot . . .
Tretiak blocks the shot . . .
. . . but Johnson is there to pick up the rebound!
Johnson shoots . . . and scores! The score is tied up at 2–2 with just one second left in the first period!

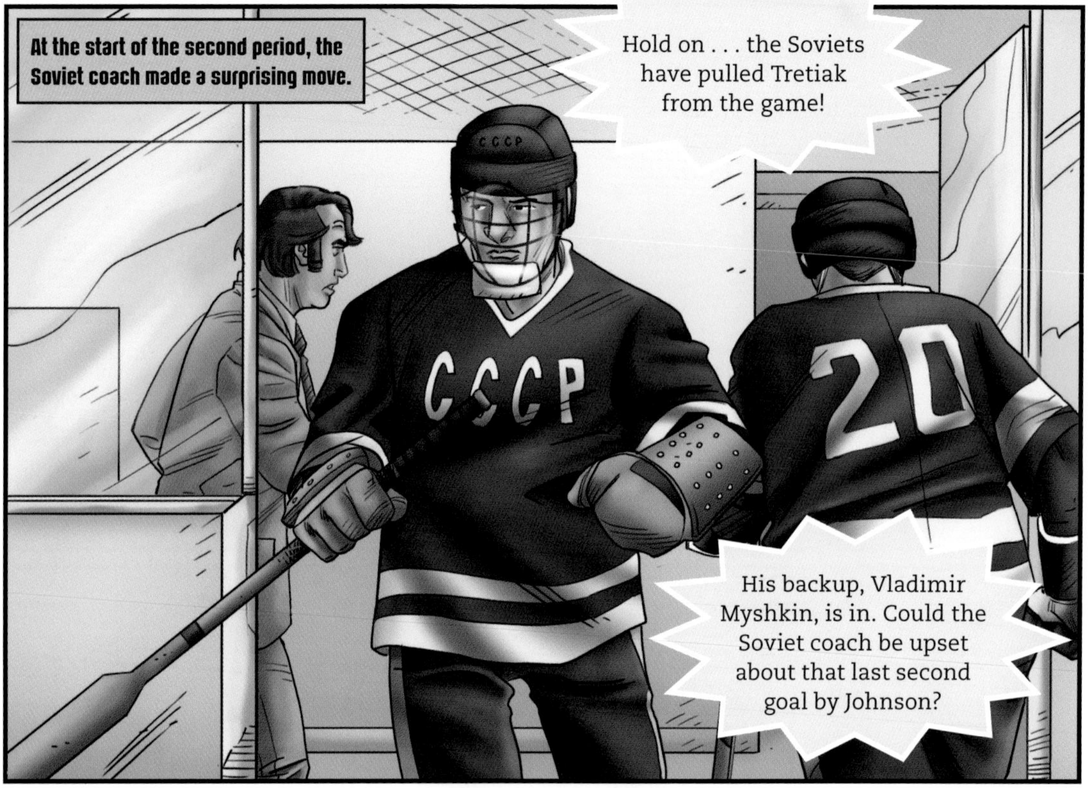
At the start of the second period, the Soviet coach made a surprising move.
Hold on . . . the Soviets have pulled Tretiak from the game!
CCCP
CCCP
20
His backup, Vladimir Myshkin, is in. Could the Soviet coach be upset about that last second goal by Johnson?

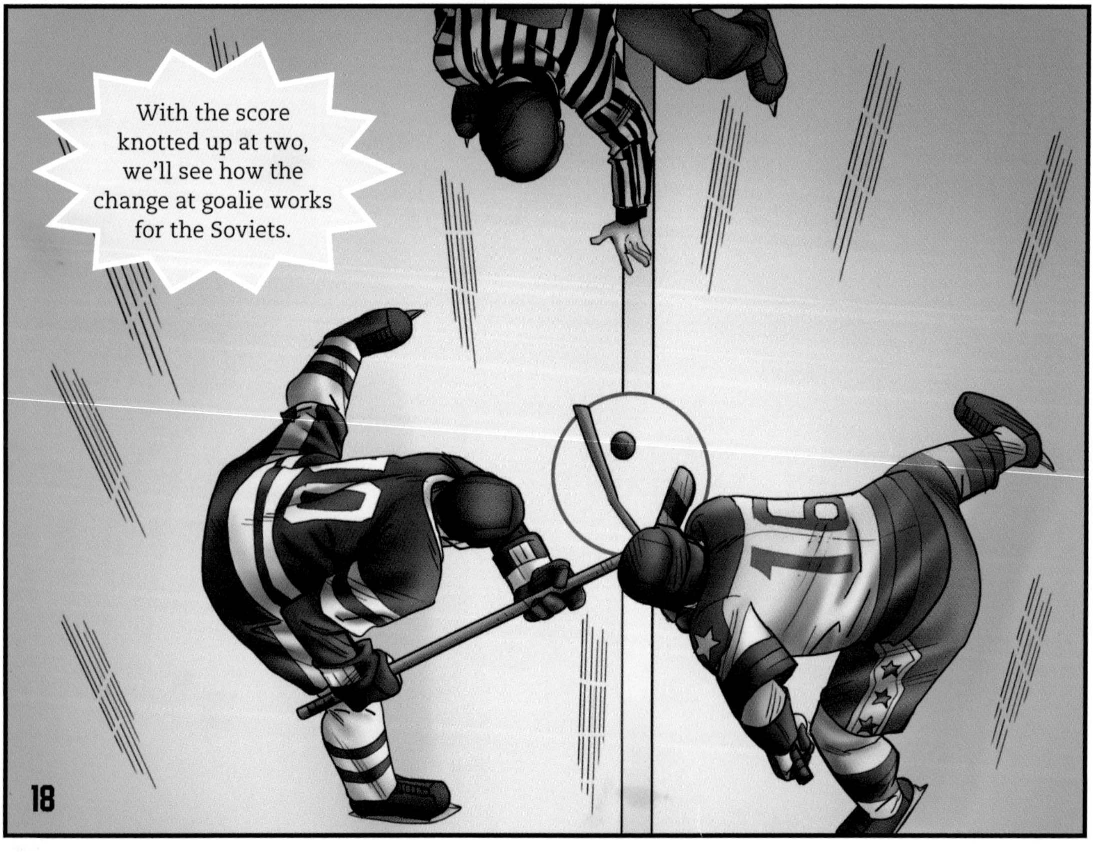
With the score knotted up at two, we'll see how the change at goalie works for the Soviets.
10
16

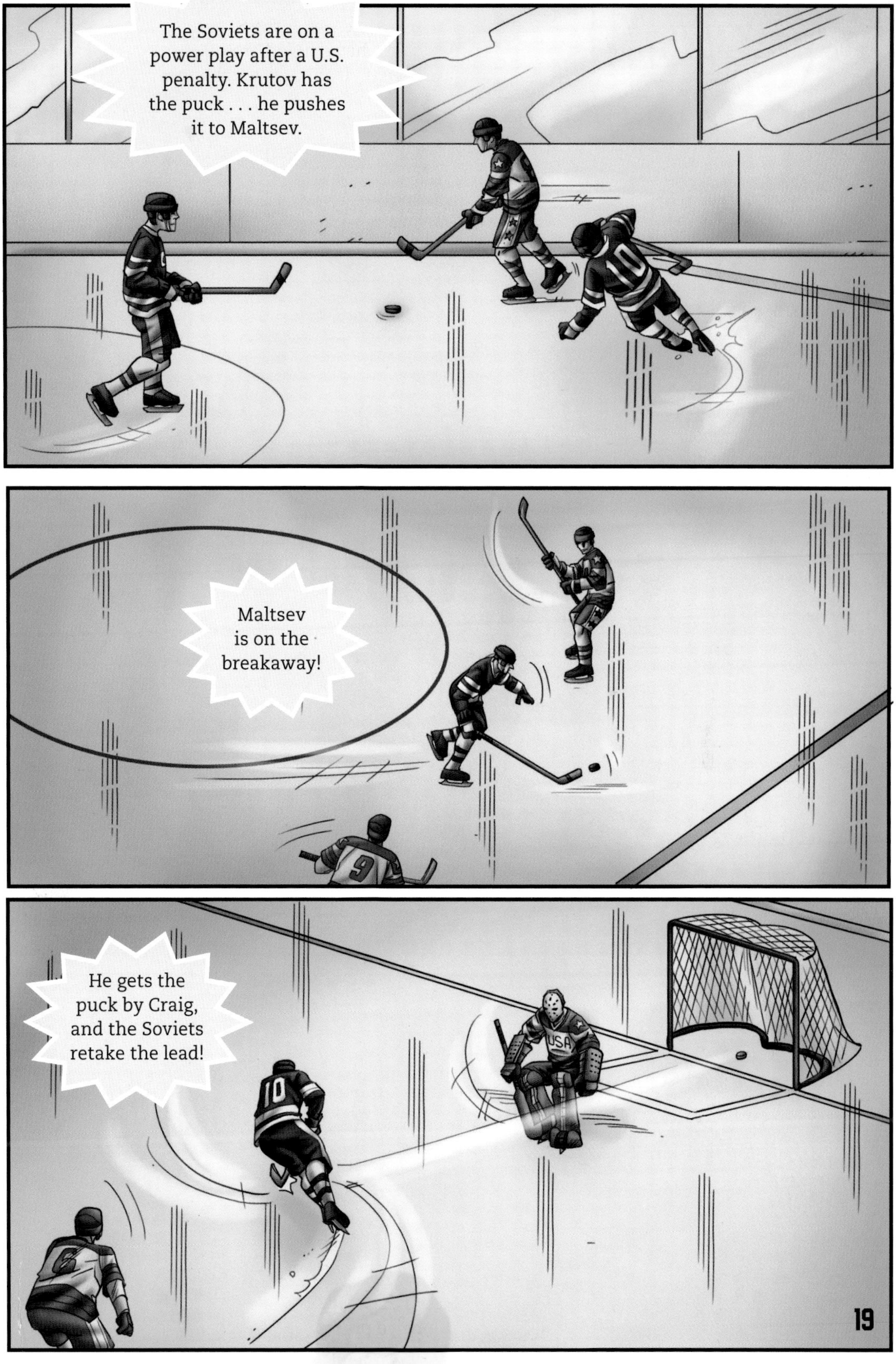
The Soviets are on a power play after a U.S. penalty. Krutov has the puck . . . he pushes it to Maltsev.
Maltsev is on the breakaway!
He gets the puck by Craig, and the Soviets retake the lead!

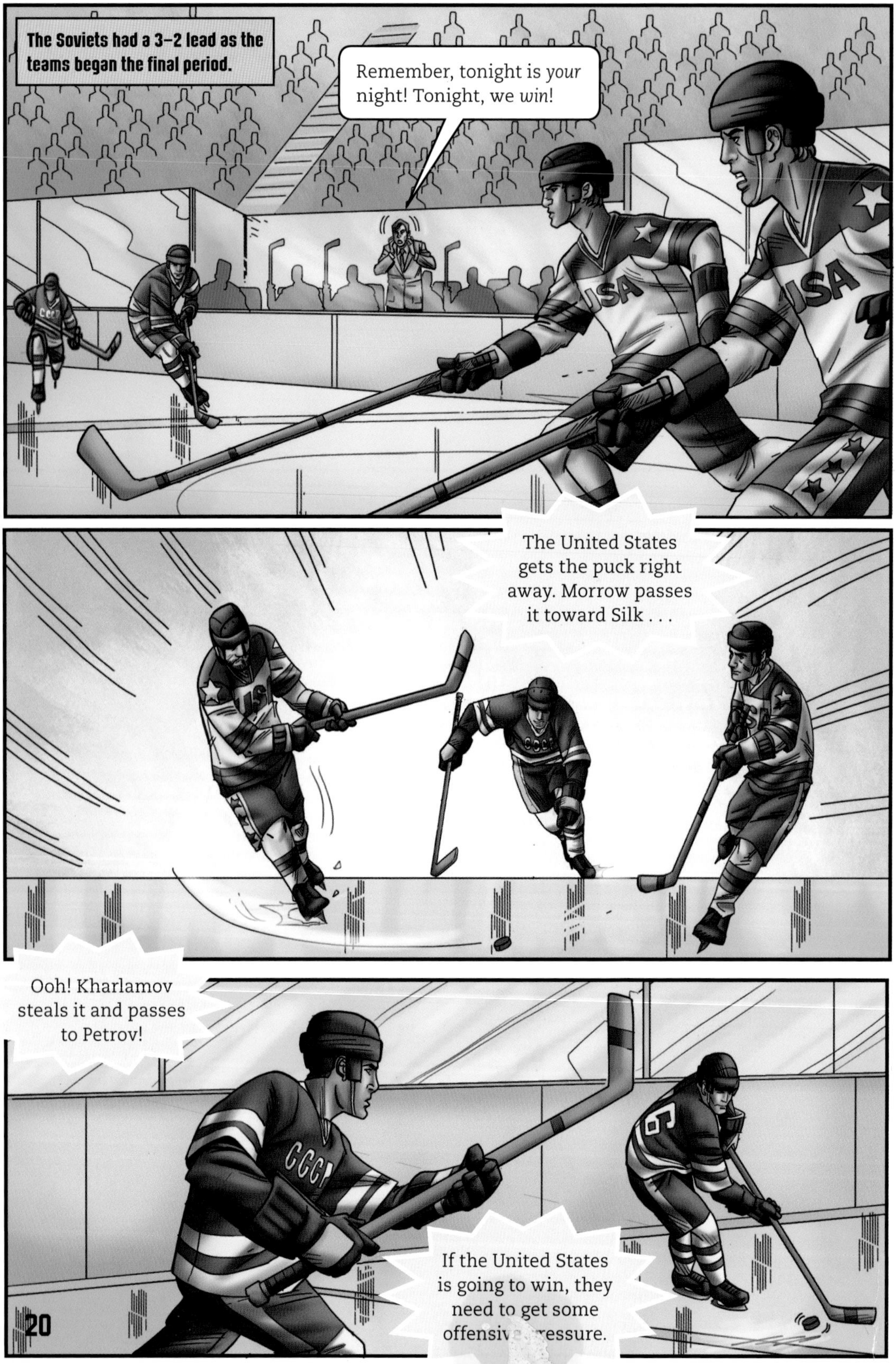
The Soviets had a 3–2 lead as the teams began the final period.
Remember, tonight is *your* night! Tonight, we *win*!
The United States gets the puck right away. Morrow passes it toward Silk . . .
Ooh! Kharlamov steals it and passes to Petrov!
If the United States is going to win, they need to get some offensive pressure.

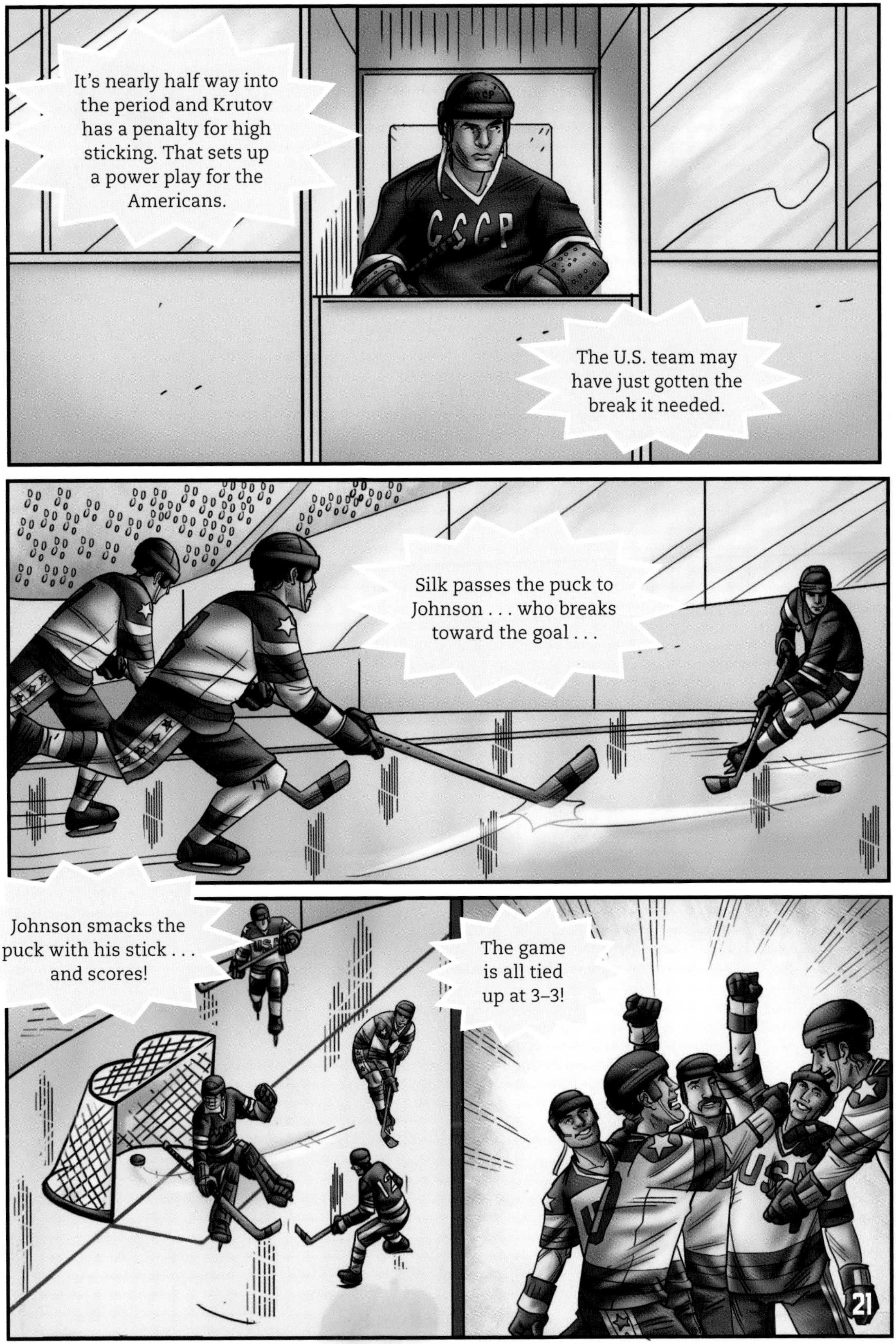
It's nearly half way into the period and Krutov has a penalty for high sticking. That sets up a power play for the Americans.
CCCP
The U.S. team may have just gotten the break it needed.
Silk passes the puck to Johnson . . . who breaks toward the goal . . .
Johnson smacks the puck with his stick . . . and scores!
The game is all tied up at 3–3!
USA

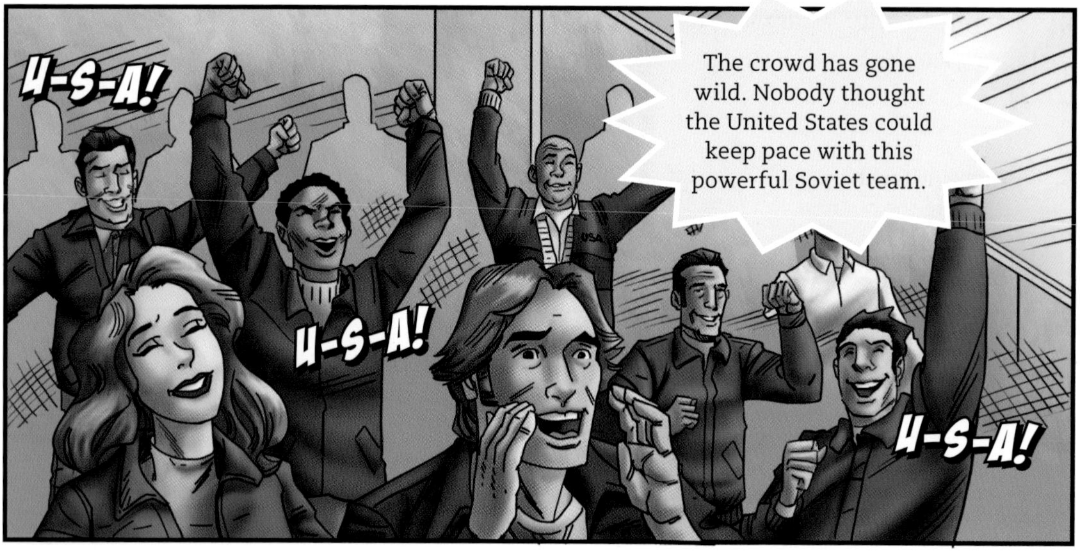
U-S-A!
The crowd has gone wild. Nobody thought the United States could keep pace with this powerful Soviet team.
U-S-A!
U-S-A!

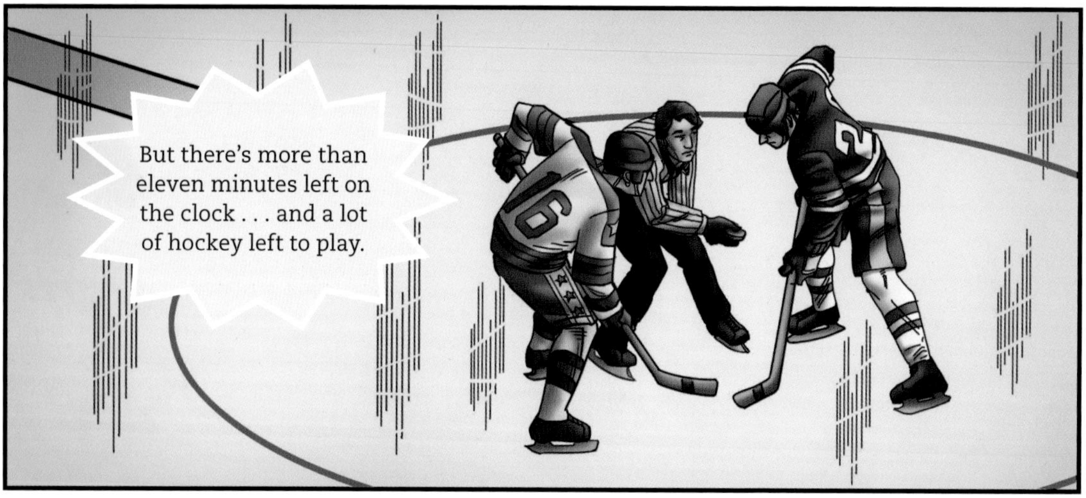
But there's more than eleven minutes left on the clock . . . and a lot of hockey left to play.

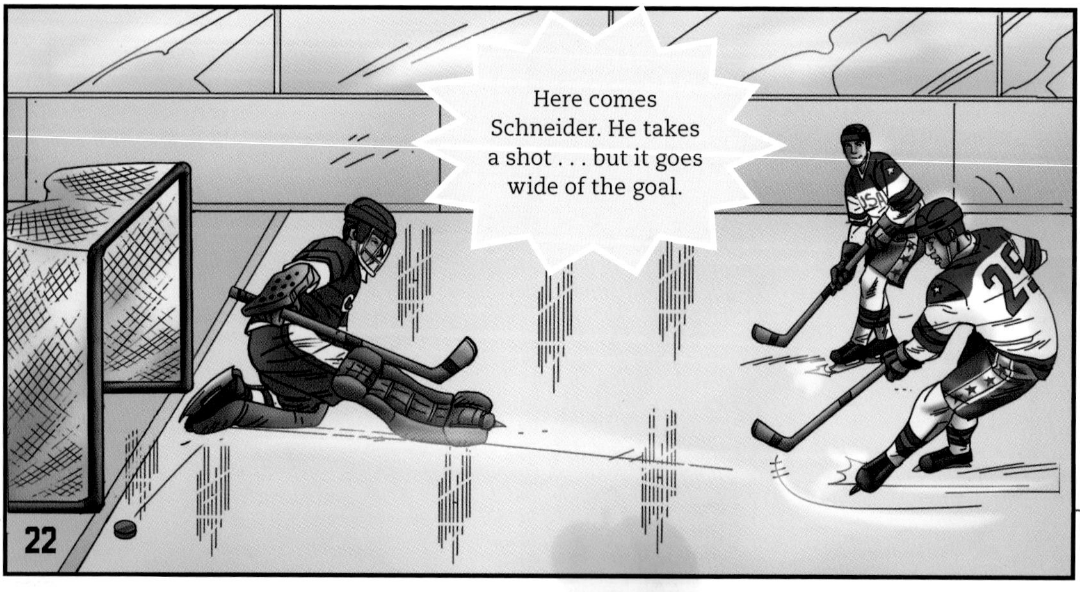
Here comes Schneider. He takes a shot . . . but it goes wide of the goal.

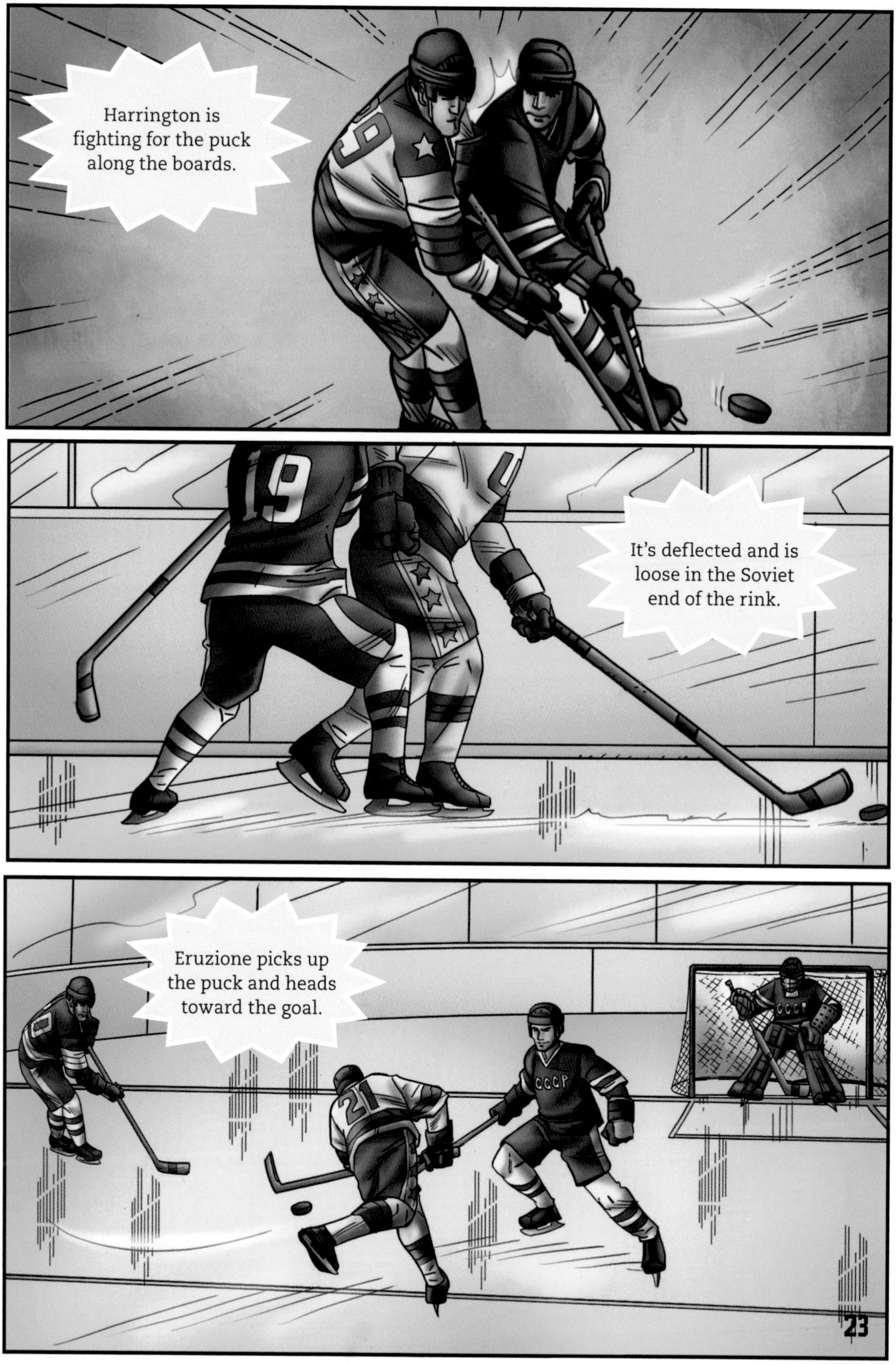
Harrington is fighting for the puck along the boards.
It's deflected and is loose in the Soviet end of the rink.
Eruzione picks up the puck and heads toward the goal.

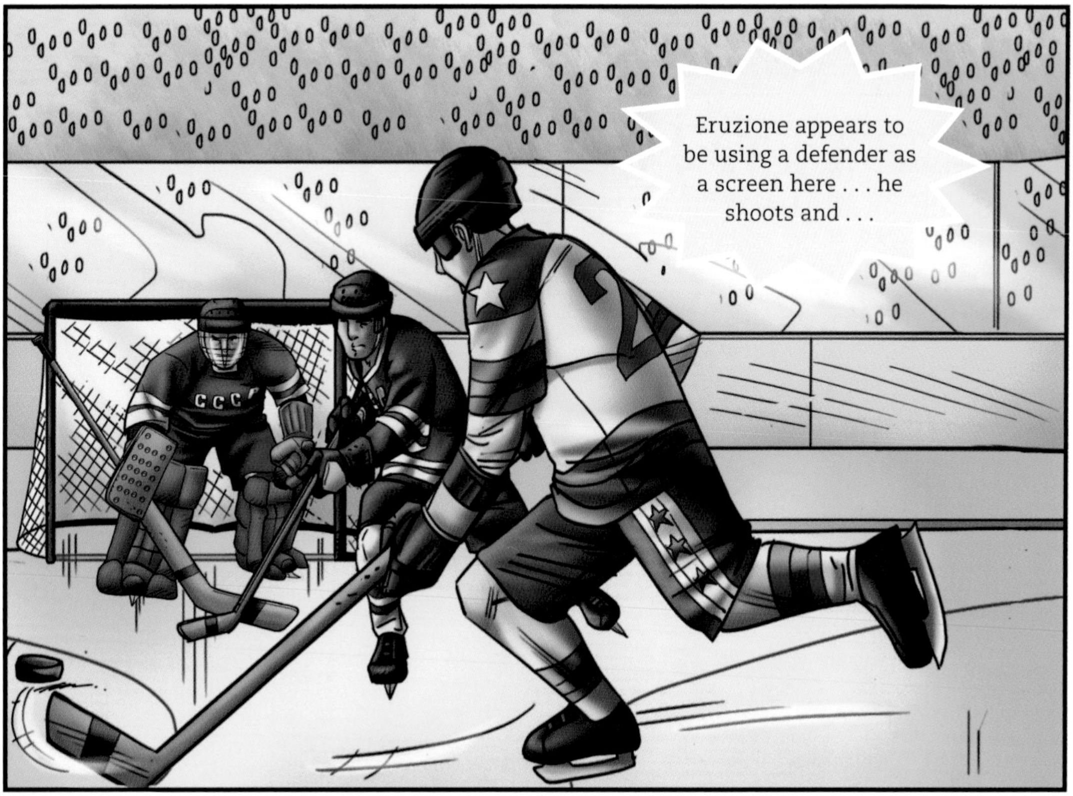
Eruzione appears to be using a defender as a screen here . . . he shoots and . . .

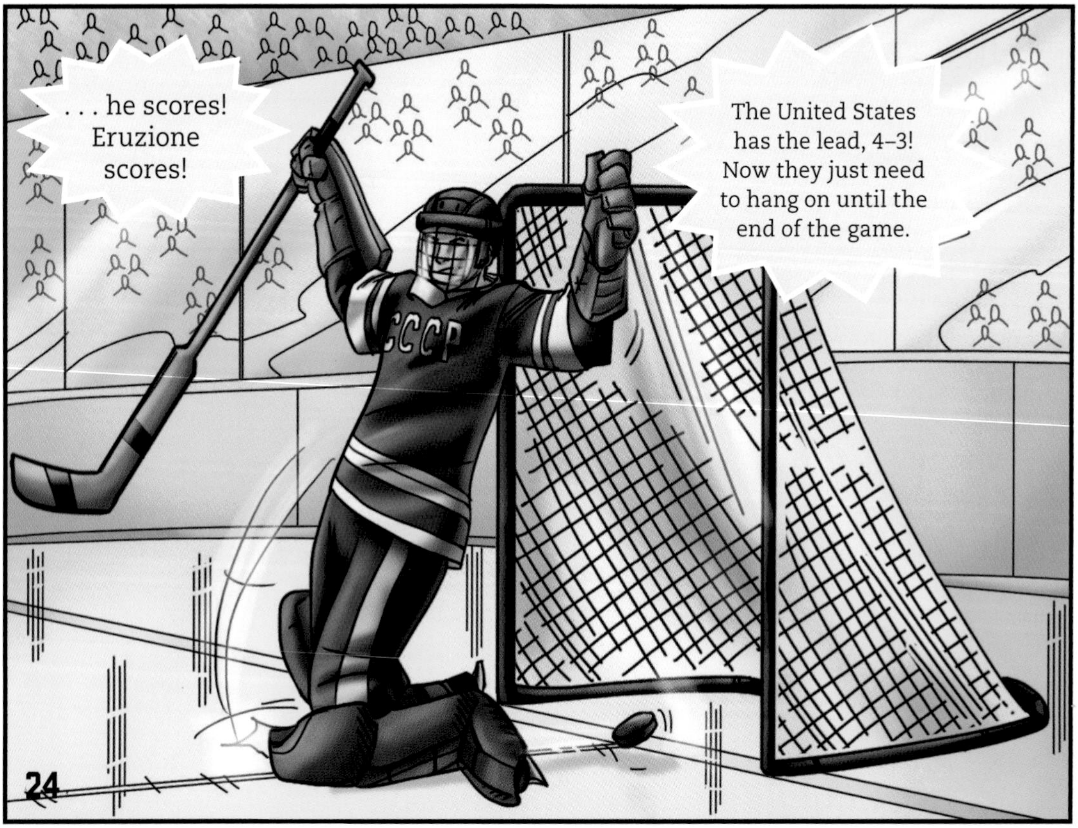
. . . he scores! Eruzione scores!
The United States has the lead, 4–3! Now they just need to hang on until the end of the game.

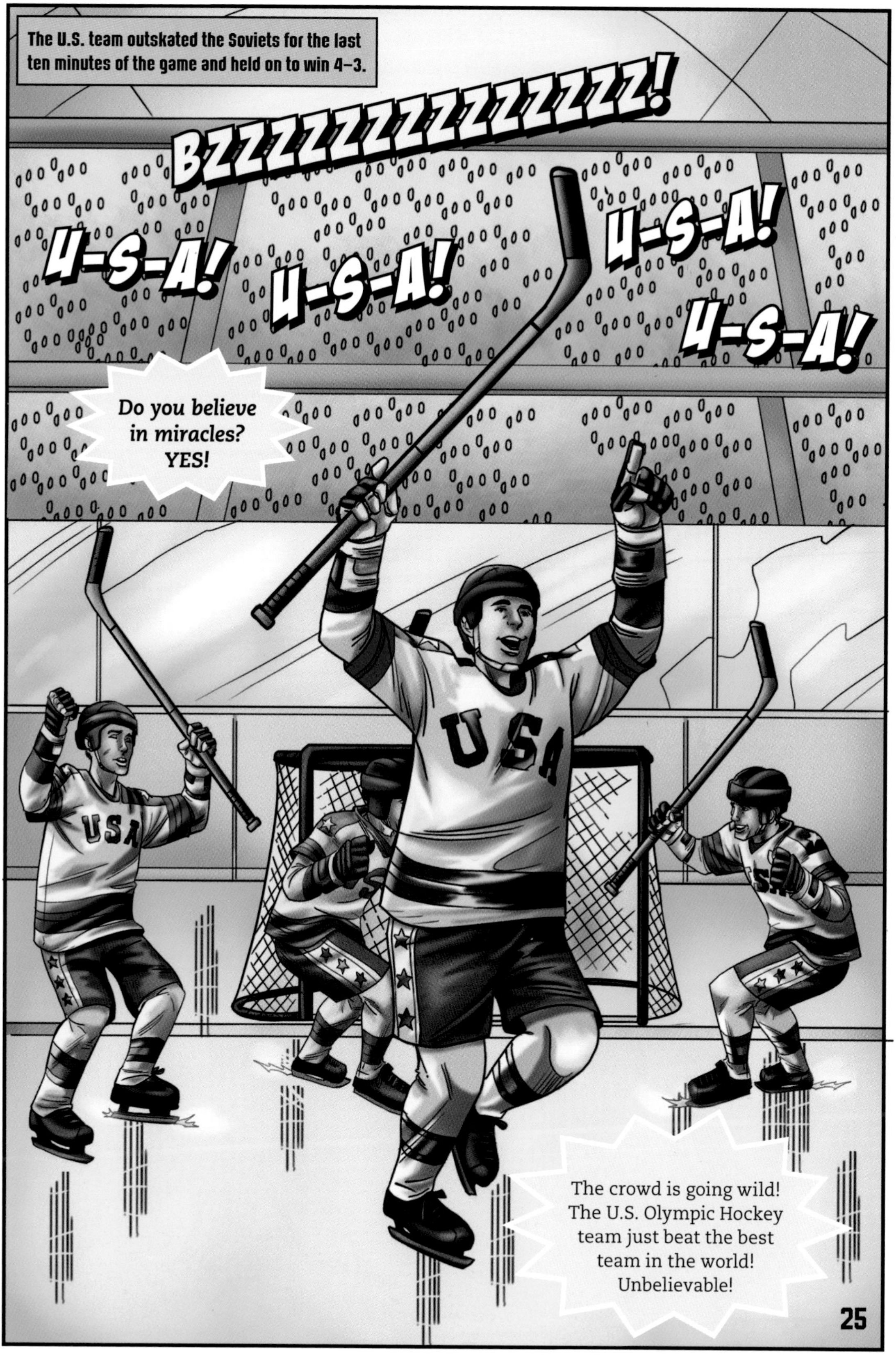

The U.S. team outskated the Soviets for the last ten minutes of the game and held on to win 4–3.
BZZZZZZZZZZZZZZZ!
U-S-A!
U-S-A!
U-S-A!
U-S-A!
Do you believe in miracles? YES!
USA
USA
USA
The crowd is going wild! The U.S. Olympic Hockey team just beat the best team in the world! Unbelievable!

WINNING IT ALL

The United States had beaten their toughest foe. But the gold medal wasn't theirs yet. They still had to face a strong Finland team.

Finland is in the power play and . . . Leinonen deflects the puck into the net. Goal!

After the second period, the U.S. team was down 2–1.

Men, we need to get it together. After beating the Soviets, *if you lose this game, you'll take it to your graves!*

Brooks sure has his team fired up. They tied it at two in the second period.

McClanahan takes the pass from Johnson . . . and scores! The U.S. is now up 3–2!

The U.S. Hockey team would score one more goal to beat Finland 4–2.

The 1980 U.S. Men's National Hockey Team had shocked the world. They did what no U.S. Olympic Hockey team had done since 1960. They beat the Soviets and went on to win Olympic gold—and the hearts of Americans everywhere.

27

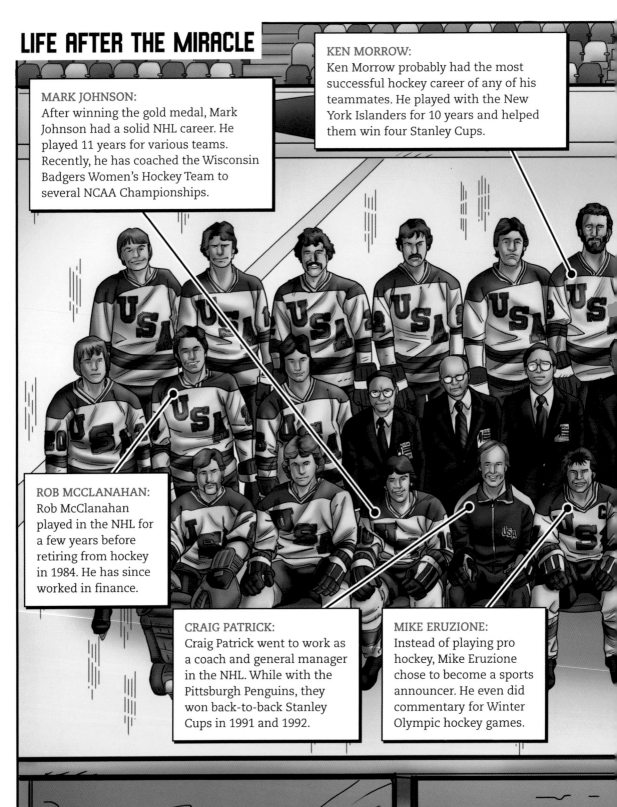

LIFE AFTER THE MIRACLE

KEN MORROW:
Ken Morrow probably had the most successful hockey career of any of his teammates. He played with the New York Islanders for 10 years and helped them win four Stanley Cups.

MARK JOHNSON:
After winning the gold medal, Mark Johnson had a solid NHL career. He played 11 years for various teams. Recently, he has coached the Wisconsin Badgers Women's Hockey Team to several NCAA Championships.

ROB MCCLANAHAN:
Rob McClanahan played in the NHL for a few years before retiring from hockey in 1984. He has since worked in finance.

CRAIG PATRICK:
Craig Patrick went to work as a coach and general manager in the NHL. While with the Pittsburgh Penguins, they won back-to-back Stanley Cups in 1991 and 1992.

MIKE ERUZIONE:
Instead of playing pro hockey, Mike Eruzione chose to become a sports announcer. He even did commentary for Winter Olympic hockey games.

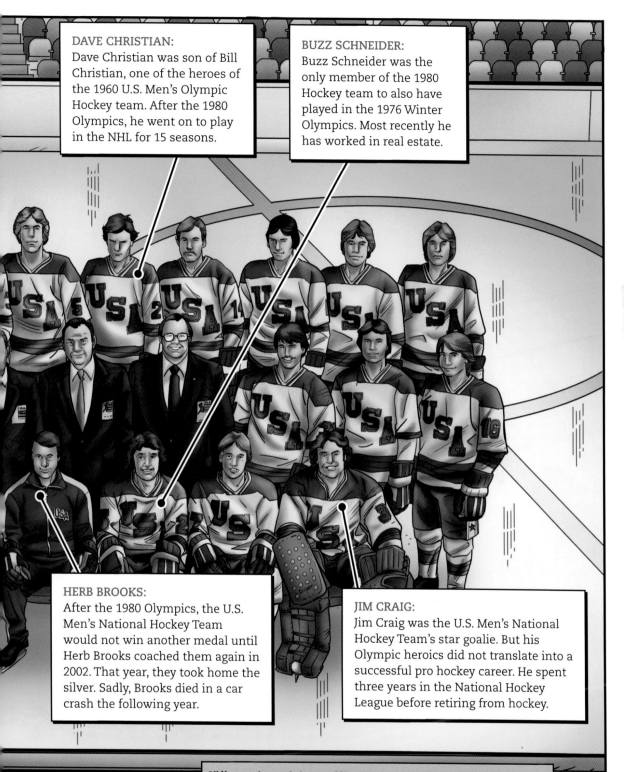

DAVE CHRISTIAN:
Dave Christian was son of Bill Christian, one of the heroes of the 1960 U.S. Men's Olympic Hockey team. After the 1980 Olympics, he went on to play in the NHL for 15 seasons.

BUZZ SCHNEIDER:
Buzz Schneider was the only member of the 1980 Hockey team to also have played in the 1976 Winter Olympics. Most recently he has worked in real estate.

HERB BROOKS:
After the 1980 Olympics, the U.S. Men's National Hockey Team would not win another medal until Herb Brooks coached them again in 2002. That year, they took home the silver. Sadly, Brooks died in a car crash the following year.

JIM CRAIG:
Jim Craig was the U.S. Men's National Hockey Team's star goalie. But his Olympic heroics did not translate into a successful pro hockey career. He spent three years in the National Hockey League before retiring from hockey.

All the coaches and players of the 1980 U.S. Men's National Hockey Team have been inducted into the U.S. Hockey Hall of Fame. *Sports Illustrated* magazine ranked the Miracle on Ice as the greatest moment ever in sports history.

GLOSSARY

amateur (AM-uh-chur)—an athlete who is not paid for playing a sport

breakaway (BRAKE-uh-way)—when a player has possession of the puck and there are no defenders other than the goalie between him and the goal

conditioning (kuhn-DISH-uhn-ing)—the act of training the body for top physical performance

contender (kuhn-TEN-dur)—someone who competes for a championship

exhibition (ek-suh-BI-shuhn)—a game or display in which someone publicly shows their skills and abilities

face-off (FAYS-off)—in hockey, when the referee drops the puck between one player from each team; the players battle for possession of the puck to start or restart play

hat trick (HAT TRIK)—when a hockey player scores three goals in one game

penalty (PEN-uhl-tee)—punishment when a player breaks the rules; the player has to sit in the penalty box for two or more minutes

period (PEER-ee-uhd)—an equal portion of playing time for an athletic game; hockey periods last 20 minutes

power play (POW-ur PLAY)—when a hockey team has a one- or two-player advantage because the other team has players in the penalty box

rebound (REE-bound)—a puck that bounces off a goalkeeper while attempting to make a save

strategy (STRAT-uh-jee)—a plan for winning a competition

READ MORE

Bradley, Michael. *Pro Hockey's Underdogs: Players and Teams Who Shocked the Hockey World.* Sports Shockers! North Mankato, Minn.: Capstone Press, 2018.

Burgan, Michael. *Miracle on Ice: How a Stunning Upset United a Country.* Captured Sports History. North Mankato, Minn.: Capstone Press, 2016.

Trusdell, Brian. *The Miracle on Ice.* Greatest Events in Sports History. Minneapolis: Abdo Publishing, 2015.

CRITICAL THINKING QUESTIONS

- Herb Brooks was the last player cut from the 1960 U.S. Men's Olympic Hockey team that won a gold medal. How might that have motivated him when preparing for the 1980 Olympics?

- In 1980 the Soviet Union was heavily favored to win the gold medal. But the U.S. Hockey team won gold by scoring just one more point than the Soviets. It was a miraculous achievement. However, if the U.S. team had lost against Finland, they wouldn't have won the gold medal. Do you think that would have made beating the Soviets any less important?

- Coach Brooks knew the U.S. team had to change its style of play to compete with teams like the Soviets. Have you ever had to change how you do something in order to succeed? Explain your answer.

INTERNET SITES

Use Facthound to find Internet sites related to this book.

Visit *www.facthound.com*

Just type in 9781543528671 and go.

Check out projects, games and lots more at
www.capstonekids.com

INDEX

Score
with
Football Math

Stuart A. P. Murray

Enslow Elementary
an imprint of
Enslow Publishers, Inc.
40 Industrial Road
Box 398
Berkeley Heights, NJ 07922
USA

http://www.enslow.com

Enslow Elementary, an imprint of Enslow Publishers, Inc.
Enslow Elementary® is a registered trademark of Enslow Publishers, Inc.

Library of Congress Cataloging-in-Publication Data

Murray, Stuart, 1948-
  Score with football math / Stuart A.P. Murray.
      pages cm. — (Score with sports math)
  Includes index.
  Summary: "Get fun football facts while practicing math techniques such as addition, subtraction, and geometry. Also includes math problem-solving tips"—Provided by publisher.
  ISBN 978-0-7660-4173-8
  1. Football—Mathematics—Juvenile literature. 2. Arithmetic—Juvenile literature. I. Title.
  GV950.7.M87 2014
  796.332092—dc23

                            2012028798

Future editions:
Paperback ISBN: 978-1-4644-0285-2   EPUB ISBN: 978-1-4645-1179-0
Single-User PDF ISBN: 978-1-4646-1179-7   Multi-User PDF ISBN: 978-0-7660-5808-8

Printed in China
012013 Leo Paper Group, Heshan City, Guangdong, China
10 9 8 7 6 5 4 3 2 1

To Our Readers: We have done our best to make sure all Internet Addresses in this book were active and appropriate when we went to press. However, the author and the publisher have no control over and assume no liability for the material available on those Internet sites or on other Web sites they may link to. Any comments or suggestions can be sent by e-mail to comments@enslow.com or to the address on the back cover.

Design and Production: Rachel D. Turetsky, Lily Book Productions

Illustration Credits: Action Sports Photography/Shutterstock.com, p. 28; Aspen Photo/ Shutterstock.com, p. 14; Brandon Laufenberg/Photos.com, p. 41; © 2012 Clipart.com, pp. 3, 5, 6, 9, 13, 15, 16, 17, 21, 22, 26, 27, 31, 32, 36, 37, 46; Debby Wong/Shutterstock.com, p. 12; giles la rock/Photos.com, p. 9; iStockphoto.com/Bill Grove, pp. 20, 33, 42, 43; Jeremy R. Smith Sr./Shutterstock.com, p. 8; Jupiterimages/Photos.com, p. 38; Ken Durden/Shutterstock.com, p. 1; Kirk Strickland/Photos.com, pp. 23, 45; Michelle Donahue Hillison/Shutterstock.com, p. 18; Olga Bogatyrenko/Shutterstock.com, p. 4; razihusin/Photos.com, p. 32; Richard Paul Kane/Shutterstock. com, pp. 34, 35; Shutterstock.com, pp. 10, 11; U.S. Air Force photo/Staff Sgt. Kristi Machado, p. 7; Wikimedia/Paul Keleher, p. 25.

Cover Photo: Shutterstock.com

Contents

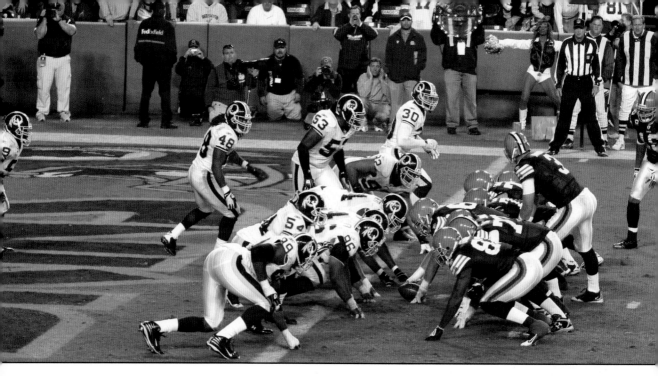

Introduction:
Hard-Hitting Tackles
and Good Math Skills

Each fall athletes in their helmets and shoulder pads
appear on football fields in every American town.
Football is rough and colorful. It thrills millions of
players and fans with its skill and excitement.

But playing football takes more than athletic skill
and strength. It also takes math. For every play,

football players have to know how many yards the offense needs to gain. They know how many points a team needs to win. Coaches have to decide what kinds of scores they need to make: touchdowns or field goals?

First downs, touchdowns, and field goals

Football teams on offense have 4 chances (downs) to gain 10 yards. If they do, they get a first down. Then they get another 4 chances to go 10 yards.

A touchdown (TD) is worth 6 points. The team can try to kick an extra point. Or the team can go for a 2-point conversion by running or throwing the ball into the end zone.

If the offense can't score a touchdown, they can try to kick a field goal, which is worth 3 points.

6+1+3=10

If a team is losing, the coach has to do some math to figure out how to win. If his team is down by 9 points, he needs a touchdown, an extra point, and a field goal: 6 + 1 + 3 = 10 points and victory!

Football math and keeping stats

Football teams are organized into squads of players with different jobs. These include offense, defense, and special teams: field goal kickers, punting specialists, kickoff teams, and kick-receiving teams.

Football players need to use math to figure out their statistics (stats), such as the quarterback's number of passes, the defense's interceptions, and the number of tackles a lineman makes. And, of course, they need to figure out which player scores the most touchdowns.

It's not just players and coaches who keep track of football stats. So do fans. It makes the game even more exciting. In this book, you'll learn some football facts and history, and you'll practice your math, too. Math helps you understand football better. And you'll find that math can be a lot of fun.

Superbowl XLIII, Tampa, Florida, 2009

The Super Bowl

The National Football League's (NFL) Super Bowl is its championship game. Each game is numbered with Roman numerals. The first (in 1967) was I, and the forty-sixth was XLVI (in 2012). The NFL Super Bowl is the most-watched sports event in the United States. More than 24 million people viewed Super Bowl I on television. For XLVI, a total of 167 million viewers tuned in all around the world.

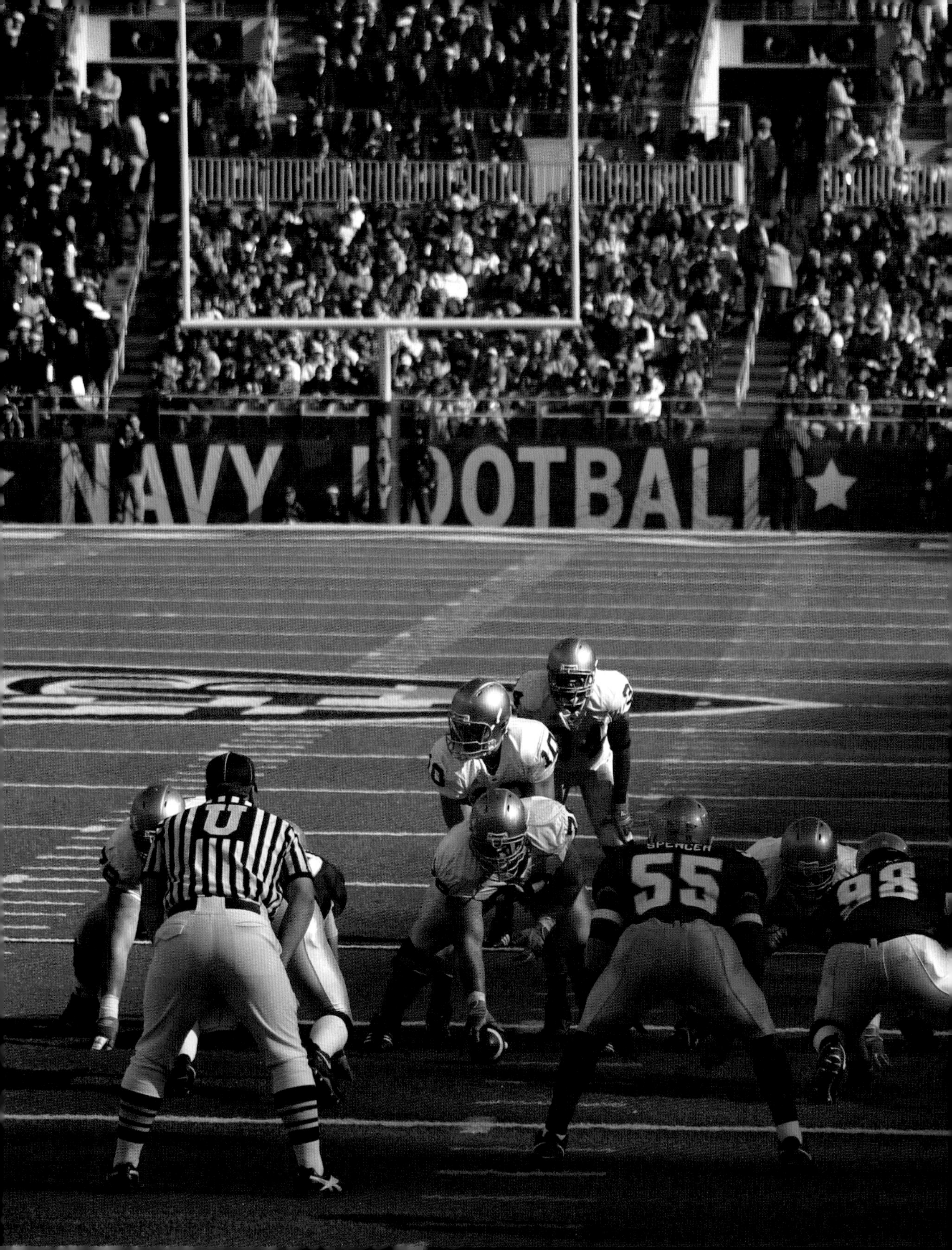
NAVY
SPENCER
55
98

1

A Hundred Yards to Score

The length of the football field from goal line to goal line is 100 yards. This is called the "playing field." It's 100 yards that can seem like 1,000 to an offense that can't move down the field. But the football field never seems long enough to a defense that's getting scored against all game.

The offense tries every way it can to break through for 10 yards and a first down. And the defense fights hard to hold on to every one of those yards and get the ball back.

10×10=100

ALL RIGHT! SCORE!

Navy's offense moves close to Notre Dame's goal line.

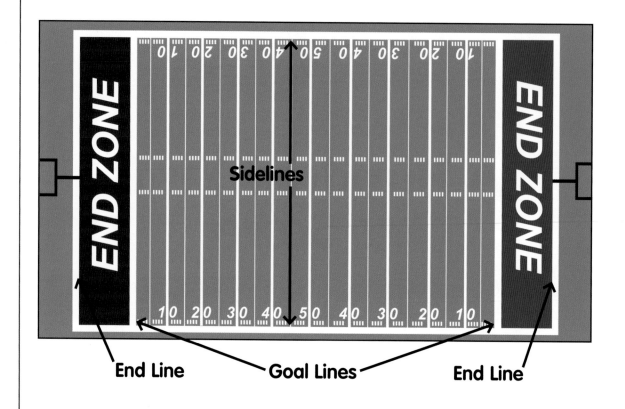

End Line   Goal Lines   End Line

A "gridiron" with end zones

There's geometry in football. The football field is a rectangle with two parallel sidelines that are each 120 yards long. The rectangle's shorter sides are the end lines, about 53 yards long.

White lines cross the playing field every 5 yards. At each end of the playing field are the goal lines.

These mark the two end zones, where teams score. The pattern of these lines gives the football field its nickname, a gridiron—a grate for grilling food.

Q: Some football field lines are marked with the numbers 10, 20, 30, 40, and 50. These are called 10-yard lines. Count how many 10-yard lines there are. How many 10-yard-wide rectangles are formed by the 10-yard lines and the sidelines?

A: There are nine 10-yard lines. There are 10 rectangles.

Q: The playing field is 100 yards long, and a yard has 3 feet. How many feet long is the playing field?

A: Multiply the number of yards (100) by 3.
100 × 3 = 300 ft.

$$\begin{array}{r} 100 \\ \times\ 3 \\ \hline 300 \end{array}$$

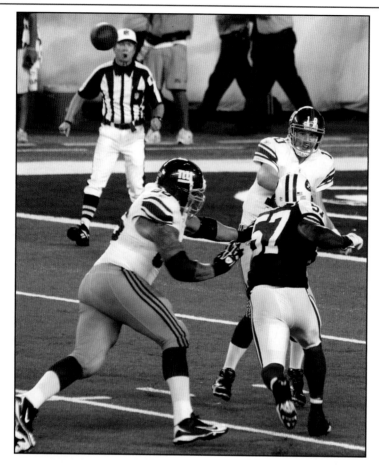

New York Giant Eli Manning passes against the New York Jets.

The real distance to a score

At the start of every down, the two teams are separated by the line of scrimmage. Complete passes and carries (runs) are measured by how many yards they go beyond the line of scrimmage before the play ends. Every pass, run, and kick actually starts several yards behind scrimmage.

Q: The ball is on the defense's 30. The quarterback throws from 7 yards behind the line and the receiver catches the ball 5 yards into the end zone. How many yards did the football travel for the touchdown?

A: Add the three figures: 7 yards to the line of scrimmage, 30 yards to the goal line, and 5 yards into the end zone.
7 + 30 + 5 = 42-yard throw

Q: The ball is on the defensive team's 45. The quarterback throws and the receiver catches the ball 30 yards from the line of scrimmage. How many yards does the offensive team still have to go to score?

A: The ball was on the 45 and was thrown 30 yards. Subtract 30 from 45 to find what yard line it is now on—the number of yards to score.
45 – 30 = 15 yards to go

First downs and penalties

Coaches decide who plays and whether to run or throw the ball. Teams with good running backs often run the football play after play. They earn first downs on the ground and keep on going to the goal line.

Referees place the ball to measure for a first down.

Q: A team goes 53 yards for a touchdown by running 10 yards on every play except for the last. How many first downs were there?

A: Gaining 10 yards earns a first down. Divide the total yards to go by 10. $53 \div 10 = 5$ first downs plus the 3 yards gained in the last play.

Referees throw bright yellow penalty flags to call penalties for mistakes or fouls. A penalty can cost a team 5, 10, or 15 yards. For example, if a defensive player crosses the line of scrimmage before the ball is hiked, his team has to move back 5 yards. Most penalties move the guilty team back toward its own end zone.

Q: A team had 8 penalties that totaled 120 yards. How many yards was each penalty?

A: Try adding combinations of 5, 10, and 15 yard penalties. You'll see it takes more than 8 different penalties to add up to 120 yards. Then, divide 120 by 8.

120 ÷ 8 = 15

So, the penalties all had to be the same: 15 yards each.

Q: This same team gained only 110 total yards in the game. Compare the total penalty yards to the total yards gained. Which symbol makes this sentence true?

120 penalty yards (?) 110 yards gained

=, <, >

A: > greater than

-5 yards
-10 yards
-15 yards

Get the clock on your side

Time-outs, fumbles, and incomplete passes stop the game's time clock, but running plays don't. Coaches who are winning near the end of a game try to run the ball. This keeps the clock ticking away the minutes.

Coaches can stop the clock with time-outs. A team is allowed to call 3 time-outs in each half, or a total of 6 time-outs (3 + 3).

Q: A coach whose team is losing late in the second half calls a time-out to stop the clock. He has used all of his first-half time-outs. How many are left?

A: He used 3 in the first half and 1 in the second.

6 − (3 + 1) = 2 time-outs left

A team is winning by just 6 points. They have the ball with 1 minute and 50 seconds left in the game.

The coach tells his players to run the ball to keep the clock going. The other team has no more time-outs.

Q: How many total seconds does the team with the ball have to use up before the final whistle?

A: Add the 60 seconds in a minute to the remaining 50 seconds.

$$60 + 50 = 110 \text{ seconds to go}$$

But the running back fumbles and the other team recovers. The clock stops, with 25 seconds used up.

Q: How many seconds are left for the other team to try to score?

A: Subtract 25 seconds from the original 110 seconds.

$$110 - 25 = 85 \text{ seconds left on the clock}$$

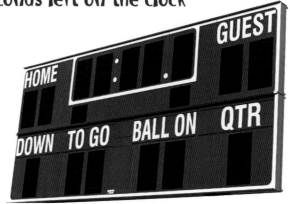

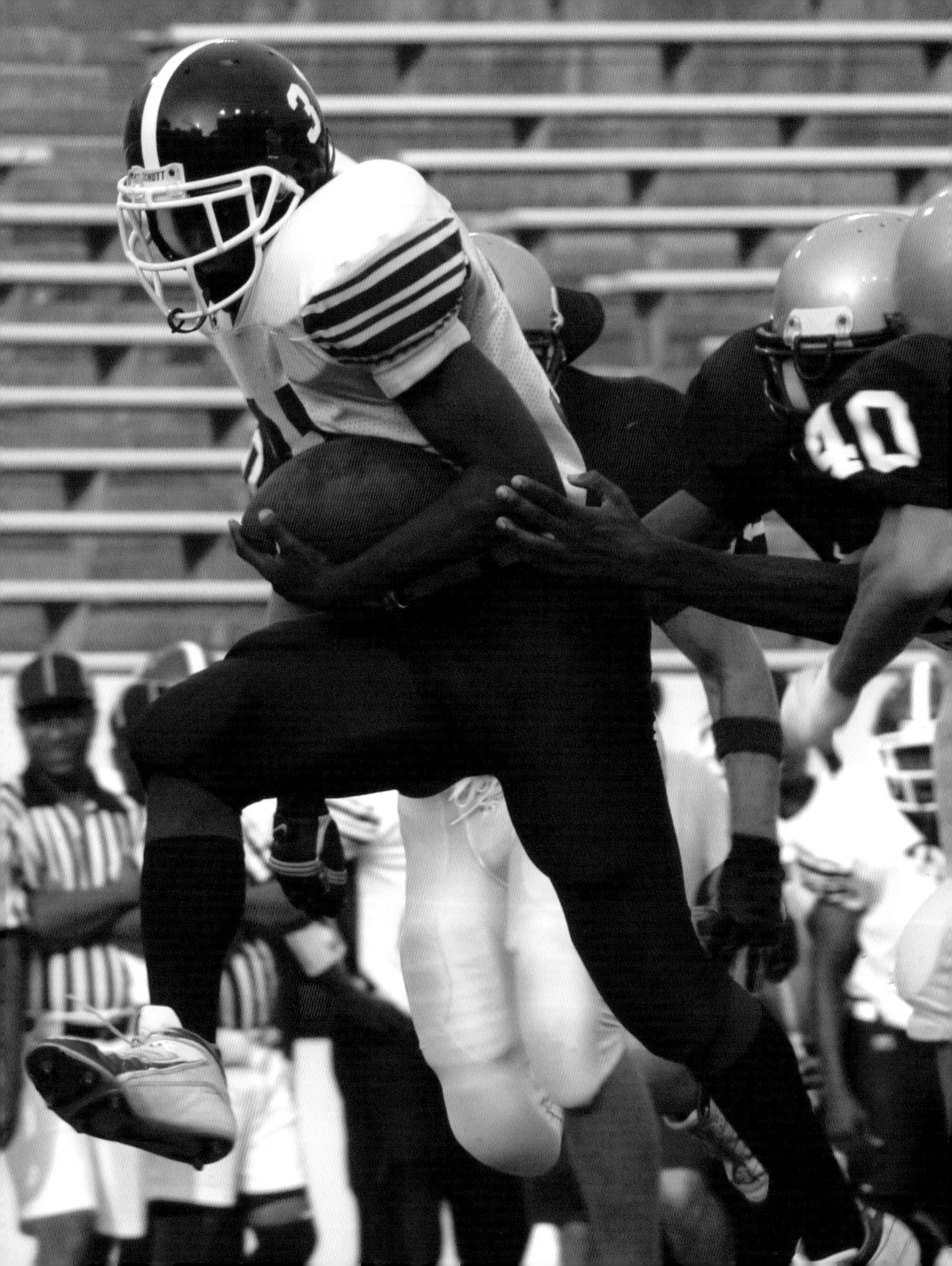
3
40

2

The Offense:
Passing, Running, and Kicking

Coaches often say "a good offense is the best defense." This means that the offensive team is on the field so much that the other team doesn't have the ball long enough to win.

Offensive stats often tell the story of the game—especially the running back's stats. A good running game usually leads to victory. When the offense runs the ball well, it uses up time on the clock. The other team's defense can't get the ball back for its offense to score.

A running back breaks through and heads for the end zone.

The offensive line

The offensive line is made up of tackles, guards, and a center. They protect the quarterback and open holes for running backs. Offensive linemen are usually smaller than defensive linemen, so they have to be quick and skillful. When the ball is snapped on running plays, offensive linemen drive the defensive linemen back. On passing plays, offensive linemen form a shield for the quarterback.

High school offensive and defensive lines get ready for the snap.

Q: The line of scrimmage is at the offensive team's 38. The line opens a hole in the defense and the running back gets to the defense's 35-yard line. How far did he run? Is it a first down?

A: The running back went from his 38 to the 50, or 12 yards. He drove on to the other team's 35, for 15 more yards.

12 + 15 = 27 total yards and a first down.

Linemen give their quarterback (QB) good protection and time to throw. The quarterback passes twice, for 14 and 16 yards. On the next play, a guard blocks a defensive lineman to open a hole for the running back. The running back scores a 12-yard touchdown.

Q: This scoring series has three downs that gain a total number of yards. In an equation, this total is the variable, (a). Write an equation and solve for (a).

A: (a) = 14 + 16 + 12

(a) = 42 yards

Passing yardage: count in the run

Quarterbacks are only as good as their receivers. The receivers include fast split ends, big and strong tight ends, and tricky running backs. Passing yardage includes how far the receiver runs with the ball after it's caught—but not any yards behind the line of scrimmage.

Q: A team has a fourth down on the opponent's 15-yard line. The quarterback throws to a running back who catches the ball 5 yards behind the line of scrimmage. He races for a touchdown. What is the total yardage of the pass?

A: The 5 yards behind the line of scrimmage are not counted. So the pass is 15 yards long.

Q: A QB throws 10 times for 158 yards. Estimate his average yardage per throw.

A: Round off 158 to 160 and divide by 10.

160 ÷ 10 = 16 yards per throw

A defensive back leaps to haul down an interception.

A quarterback can pass for a lot of yardage, but his team can still lose. This is because the more he throws, the more chances there are for the other team to intercept the ball.

Sometimes the interception is run back for a touchdown. To calculate a quarterback's passing yards, the runback yardage is subtracted from the completion yardage.

Q: A quarterback threw 12 complete passes for 200 yards. He threw 4 incomplete passes. He also threw 3 interceptions that were run back for a total of 50 yards. What was the quarterback's total passing yardage?

A: The incomplete passes are extra information in this problem, since no yards were lost. Subtract the 50 yards of interception runbacks from the quarterback's completion total of 200 yards.
200 − 50 = 150 total yards passing

The super passers of the NFL

Passing for more than 300 total yards in a game is impressive. But 119 pro quarterbacks have passed for more than 400 yards in a game. Another 12 have thrown for more than 500 yards in a game. They are listed in the chart.

NFL Quarterbacks Who Passed for More Than 500 Yards in a Game

Player	Team/Year	Yards
Norm Van Brocklin	Los Angeles Rams/1951	554
Warren Moon	Houston Oilers/1990	527
Boomer Esiason	Arizona Cardinals/1996	522
Dan Marino	Miami Dolphins/1988	521
Matthew Stafford	Detroit Lions/2012	520
Tom Brady	New England Patriots/2011	517
Phil Simms	New York Giants/1985	513
Drew Brees	New Orleans Saints/2006	510
Vince Ferragamo	Los Angeles Rams/1982	509
Y.A. Tittle	New York Giants/1962	505
Elvis Grbac	Kansas City Chiefs/2000	504
Ben Roethlisberger	Pittsburgh Steelers/2009	503

New England quarterback Tom Brady throws from the pocket formed by his teammates against the Miami Dolphins rushers.

Q: Which QB had the most yards? How many more than 400 did he throw for?

A: Van Brocklin. Subtract 400 from his total of 554.

554 − 400 = 154

Q: Which decade had the most games with more than 500 yards gained?

A: Look at the years listed and figure out whether they are in the decade of the 1950s, 1960s, 1980s, 1990s, 2000s, or 2010s.

The 1980s and 2000s had 3 games each.

Offensive weapons: the run and the kick

A good running back gains yardage play after play. When the quarterback mixes up running plays with passes, it confuses the defense.

Q: A running back gains 3 and then 4 yards. Next, the quarterback throws a completion. In these three plays, the team gains a total of 14 yards. How many yards (z) did the completed pass gain?

A: Add the running yardage and subtract from 14.

$z = 14 - (3 + 4)$

$z = 7$ yards gained by the pass

Q: After 9 seasons, a running back has averaged 850 yards each season. How many total yards did he gain?

A: $9 \times 850 = 7{,}650$ yards in 9 years

The 3 points from a field goal often decide who wins a close game. Field goal distances start from where the ball is kicked and include the 10 yards of the end zone.

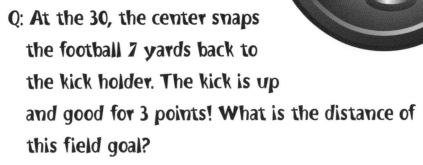

Q: At the 30, the center snaps the football 7 yards back to the kick holder. The kick is up and good for 3 points! What is the distance of this field goal?

A: Add 30 and 7 to find that the kick was made from 37 yards. Add 10 yards for the end zone.
7 + 30 + 10 = 47 yards

Q: In 7 games, a kicker had 3 field goals per game. How many total points did he score?

A: A field goal is worth 3 points, so:
3 field goals × 3 points = 9 points per game
7 games × 9 points per game = 63 points

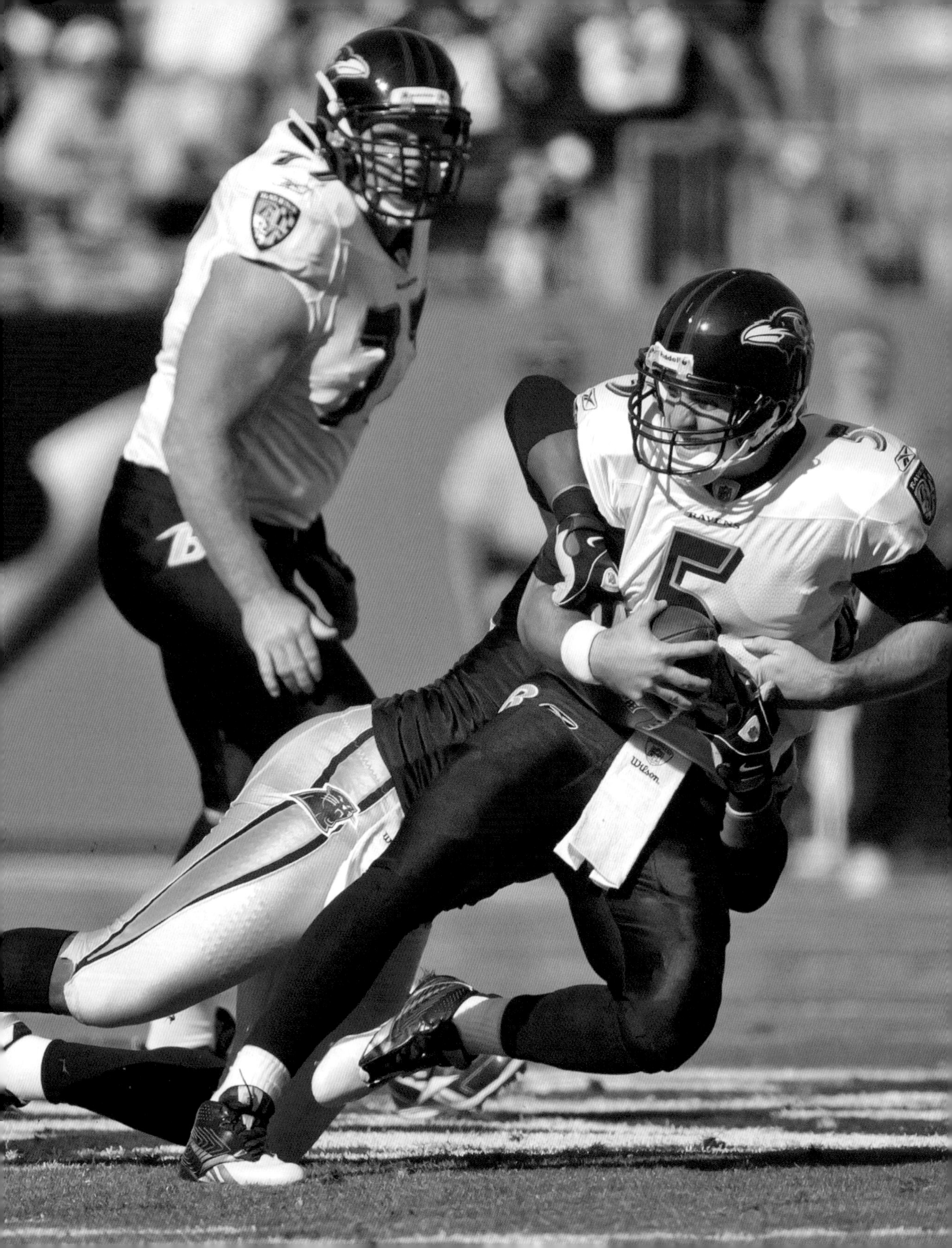
RAVENS
Wilson

3

The Defense:
Linemen, Linebackers, and Defensive Backs

Most good football teams are built around their defense. Top defenses seem to always get the ball back for their teams. They make it hard for the other team to play well.

The defense has to know exactly how many yards the other team needs for a first down or a score. The defense guesses what the opponent will do next. Defensive linemen are ready to stop the running back before he gets started. Defensive backfield players knock down passes. They also tackle running backs.

Baltimore Ravens quarterback Joe Flacco gets sacked by the Carolina Panthers.

How good is the defensive team?

Defensive stats include each player's number of tackles, interceptions, and fumbles recovered. An entire team's defensive ability is measured by how many yards per game (YPG) it gives up.

Best Defensive Teams in 2011

Team/Year	YPG
1. Houston Texans	263
2. Baltimore Ravens	322
3. New York Giants	328
4. Cincinnati Bengals	340
5. New England Patriots	348
6. New Orleans Saints	409
7. San Francisco 49ers	412
8. Green Bay Packers	420
9. Atlanta Falcons	442
10. Pittsburgh Steelers	447

The top 10 NFL defensive teams in 2011 according to the average number of yards they allowed per game (YPG).

Q: How many more YPG
did the tenth team allow
than the first team?

A: Subtract 263 from 447.

447 − 263 = 184 yards more

Q: How many teams allowed less than 400 YPG?
What fraction of the total number of teams in
the chart is this?

A: 5 teams: $\frac{5}{10}$; reduce the fraction to $\frac{1}{2}$

Q: Express in words what fraction of the total
number of teams allowed less than 300 YPG.

A: Only 1 team out of 10 allowed less than
300 YPG, so: $\frac{1}{10}$ = one tenth

Q: In the tenth team's YPG stat, which digit is
in the hundreds place? The tens place?
The ones place?

A: The Pittsburgh Steelers are tenth. Their yards
per game (YPG) total was 447.
The first 4 is in the hundreds place. The second
4 is in the tens. The 7 is in the ones.

Counting tackles and downs

Linebackers play behind (in back of) the defensive line. They try to tackle the ball carriers breaking through the line and to cover receivers trying to get open for a short pass.

Q: **Three linebackers make a total of 21 tackles in a game. What is the average number of tackles per linebacker?**

A: Divide 21 by 3.

$21 \div 3 = 7$ tackles per linebacker

Q: **A defensive line allowed 64 running yards on 8 plays. Use two different methods to find the average yardage of each play.**

A: One way is to divide 64 by 8.

$64 \div 8 = 8$ yards average per play

Another way is to use multiplication tables to find which number times 8 equals 64.

$8 \times ? = 64$

$8 \times 8 = 64$

8 yards average per play

Defenders stop the ball carrier's drive for extra yards.

When a team keeps the ball for several downs, this is called a series of downs.

Q: In each of 3 series, a defensive team made 5 tackles in running plays, allowed 3 completed passes, and knocked down 2 more passes. How many plays were there in the 3 series?

A: Multiply 3 series of downs times the total number of running plays, completes, and incompletes.

$3 \times (5 + 3 + 2) = ?$

$3 \times 10 = 30$ total plays

Defenders and kicking

Defensive teams defend against kicks. One of the hardest jobs is to block an extra point. Even though it is only one point, those points can add up.

The holder is important to getting off the kick.

Q: A defense has allowed 3 touchdowns and 2 field goals, but blocked 2 of 3 extra-point attempts. How many points did it allow?

A: 7 + 6 + 6 + 3 + 3 = 25

Q: A team scored 36 touchdowns in one season, but its kicker only made two thirds of his extra points. How many points did he score? How many did he miss?

A: First find one third of 36 by dividing 36 by 3.

$36 \div 3 = 12$

Multiply the answer by 2 to find two thirds of 36.

$12 \times 2 = 24$ points scored

Then subtract that result from the total extra point attempts.

36 − 24 = 12 points missed

A punt is not measured by how far the ball is kicked. The punt's "net distance" is measured from the line of scrimmage to where the kick receiver is tackled or goes out of bounds.

Q: The punter kicks with the line of scrimmage at his own 40. The punt returner catches the ball on his 20 and is tackled on his own 45. What is the net distance of the punt?

A punter is about to kick the ball deep into the other team's half.

A: The punt returner ran 25 yards before being tackled. Figure out the yards from the punter's 40 to the other team's 45.

50 − 40 = 10 yards

50 − 45 = 5 yards

10 + 5 = 15 yard distance for the punt

The last line of defense

The fastest defensive backs are the safeties and cornerbacks. It's their job to stay with the receivers going out for passes. They also are the last line of defense against ball carriers who have burst past the line and linebackers.

Q: Two defensive backs together had a total of 9 interceptions. One had 3 more interceptions than the other. How many did each back have?

A: Figure out what numbers add up to 9. Then subtract to see which two numbers have a difference of 3.

6 + 3 = 9

6 − 3 = 3

One had 6 interceptions and the other had 3.

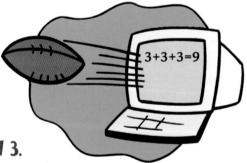

3+3+3=9

Q: Two defensive
   backs each sack the
   quarterback 3 times.
   He loses 5 yards each time.
   How much total yardage
   did the quarterback lose?

A: Multiply 2 times the number of
   sacks each back had.
   $2 \times 3 = 6$ sacks
   Then multiply 6 sacks by the yards lost.
   $6 \times 5 = 30$ total yards lost

Q: A defensive team allows 200 yards in 20
   passing plays. They allow 120 yards in 10
   running plays. Did passing or running gain
   more average yards per play?

A: $200 \div 20 = 10$ yards average per passing play
   $120 \div 10 = 12$ yards average per running play
   Running plays gained more average yards (12)
   per play than passing did (10).

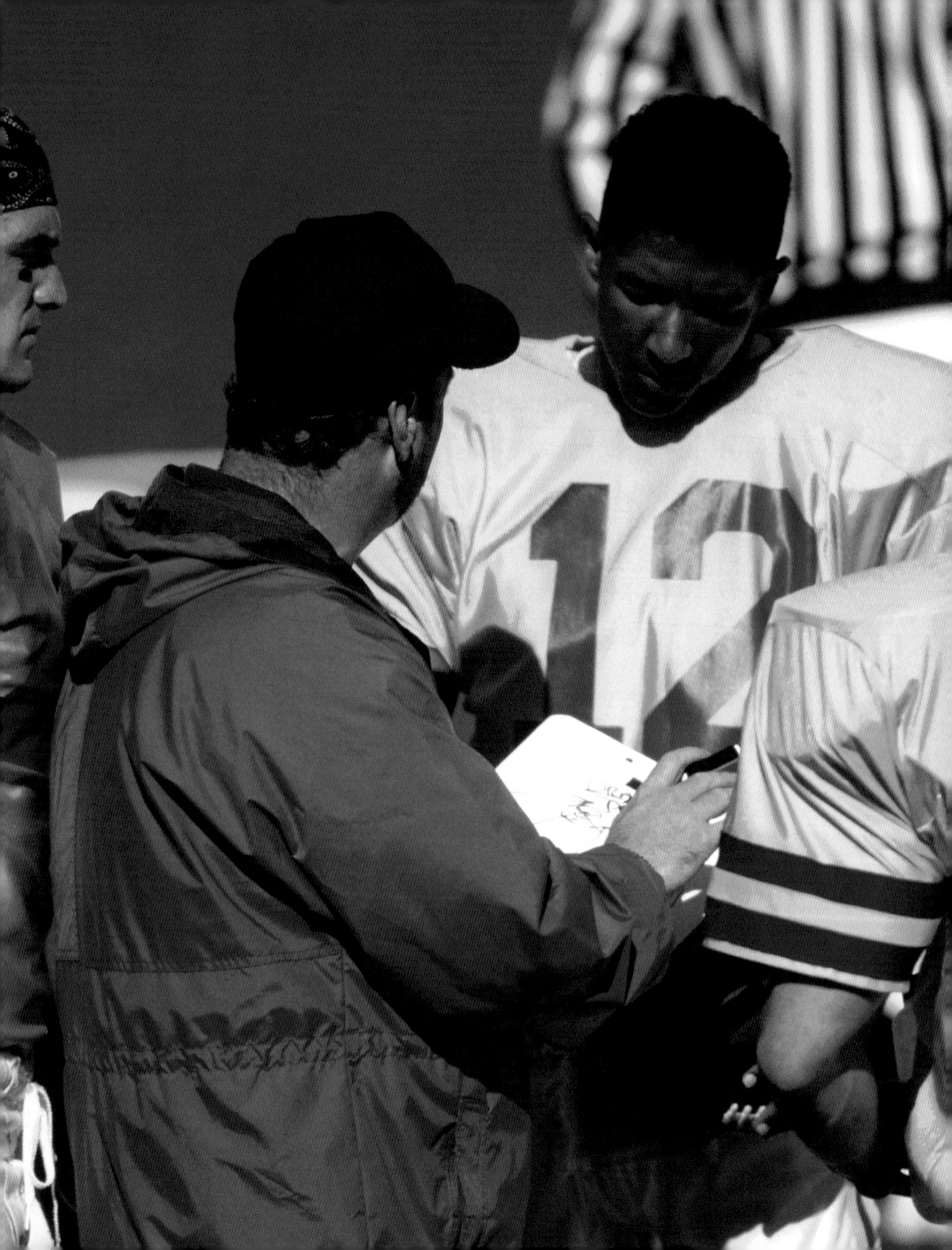

4

Coach's Last Game

The Long Valley League's winningest head coach will retire after this final game. Coach Williams always has winning football teams at Washington High.

They don't score a lot of points, but defense is their best weapon. This season, they've won every game by one touchdown or less.

Coach Johnson has a top offense at Adams High. His team has outscored everybody by at least four touchdowns. Both teams have won the same number of games. This is their last game. Whoever wins will be league champ. Can a great defense stop a great offense?

During a timeout, the coach decides on the next play.

The winningest NFL coaches

Before big games, Coach Williams likes to watch videos of great NFL coaches. Some of them were at work long before he was born.

The Winningest NFL Coaches

	Name	Wins–Losses–Ties	Years
1.	Don Shula	328-156-6	1963–95
2.	George Halas	318-148-31	1920–67
3.	Tom Landry	250-162-6	1954–88
4.	Curley Lambeau	226-132-22	1921–53
5.	Paul Brown	213-104-9	1946–75
6.	Marty Schottenheimer	200-126-1	1977–2006
7.	Chuck Noll	193-148-1	1969–91
8.	Dan Reeves	190-165-2	1977–2003
9.	Chuck Knox	186-147-1	1973–94
10.	Bill Parcells	172-130-1	1979–2006

NFL coaches with the most career victories (not including playoffs).

Q: Which great coach started in the NFL first?
A: George Halas, in 1920.

Q: Which coach had the most combined losses and ties?

A: Study the chart and guess which total might be the highest. Then add up the ones you choose. Compare the totals. Halas had the most losses and ties: 179.

Kickoff!

In the big game with Adams High, Coach Williams finds his team up against a top running back.

The QB shouts signals just before the snap.

Q: In one series, the Adams halfback runs 3 times and gains 5 yards each time. How many first downs did he get?

A: One first down with the first 2 runs:

5 yards + 5 yards = 10 yards

The fourth time he runs, he gains 9 yards and scores a touchdown. But they miss the extra point. Adams 6–Washington 0.

The Washington High defense bends

Great defenses "bend but don't break." This means that the other team gains yards and has lots of downs, but can't score very often. Late in the second half, Coach Johnson's star halfback has gained 141 yards with 14 runs, but no more touchdowns.

Q: Estimate his average gain per run.
A: Round off to 140 and divide by 14 runs.

$140 \div 14 = 10$ yards average per run

Washington has to punt, and Adams goes on offense again. Then a Washington linebacker tackles the Adams quarterback in his own end zone for a safety worth 2 points.

Adams 6–Washington 2.

The halfback's torn jersey shows he has just broken away from a tackler.

Defensive players gang-tackle the running back.

With about a minute left in the game, the Washington defense stops Adams 35 yards from another score.

Adams will try a field goal. The kicker's previous longest kick was from the 40-yard line. Now the ball is on the 35, and it will be hiked back another 7 yards.

Q: Can he make the kick?

A: Maybe. 35 yards + 7 yards = 42 yards, or 2 yards farther than his best kick ever.

The kick is good! Adams 9–Washington 2.

The 2-point conversion

Adams kicks off with 40 seconds left. The crowd goes wild when the Washington kick returner breaks through all the way to the Adams 8-yard line. They have four downs to score a touchdown!

Q: But will a touchdown and an extra point win the game?

A: Add the 2 points Washington already has to the 6 for a touchdown and 1 for an extra point:

2 + (6 + 1) = 2 + 7 = 9 points

9 points would only tie with Adams.

The Washington QB throws three times, all incomplete. But this stops the clock. Then, on fourth down, with 15 seconds left, the halfback catches a short pass. He turns and dives in for the score! Adams 9–Washington 8.

44

The running back leaps into the end zone for a touchdown.

Q: If Coach Williams wants to win, what play must he call?

A: Washington has to go for a 2-point conversion. But if they fail, the coach will lose his last game.

The Washington kicking team fakes the extra point kick. Instead, the holder sprints around the right end for 2 points—and the victory!

Washington 10–Adams 9.

Math Problem-Solving Tips

✏ Always read the problem completely before beginning to work on it.

✏ Make sure you understand the question.

✏ Some problems take more than one step to find the final answer.

✏ Don't think you always have to use every number in the problem. Some numbers are extra information that are not needed for the calculations.

✏ If you know your answer is wrong but can't find the mistake, then start again on a clean sheet of paper.

✏ Don't get upset! You can solve problems better when you're calm.

✏ If you're stuck on a problem, skip it and go on with the rest of them. You can come back to it.

Further Reading

Books

Connolly, Sean. *The Book of Perfectly Perilous Math.*
New York: Workman Publishing Company, 2012.

Fitzgerald, Theresa. *Math Dictionary for Kids.* Waco, Tex.:
Prufrock Press, Inc., 2011.

The Complete Book of Math, Grades 3 and 4.
Greensboro, N.C.: American Education Publishing, 2009.

Web Sites

Drexel University. The Math Forum @ Drexel University.
© 1994–2012.
<http://www.mathforum.org/k12/mathtips>
K–12 math problems, puzzles, and tips and tricks. The Math
Forum of Drexel University is a leading online resource for
improving math learning, teaching, and communication.

Livebinders. Football Math and Other Activities.
<http://www.livebinders.com/play/play_or_edit?id=205619>
Football math and other activities including computer football
word problems and "bug football." Students, teachers, and
parents can play with math, problem-solving, cryptograms,
and mazes.

Index